# LEOPARDI

THE LOCKERT LIBRARY OF POETRY IN TRANSLATION

EDITORIAL ADVISOR: RICHARD HOWARD

*For other titles in the Lockert Library*
*see page 91*

# LEOPARDI

## Selected Poems

Translated by Eamon Grennan

PRINCETON UNIVERSITY PRESS

· PRINCETON · NEW JERSEY ·

Copyright © 1997 by Princeton University Press

Published by Princeton University Press, 41 William Street,

Princeton, New Jersey 08540

In the United Kingdom and the Republic of Ireland: Dedalus Press, Dublin, Ireland

Library of Congress Cataloging-in-Publication Data

Leopardi, Giacomo, 1798–1837.

[Poems. English. Selections]

Leopardi : selected poems / translated by Eamon Grennan.

p.   cm.—(The Lockert library of poetry in translation)

ISBN 0-691-01643-7 (cloth : alk. paper).—ISBN 0-691-01644-5

(pbk. : alk. paper) 1. Leopardi, Giacomo, 1798–1837—Translations into English.

I. Grennan, Eamon, 1941– . II. Title. III. Series.

PQ4709.E5A13 1997    96-47721

851.7—dc21

This book has been composed in Dante

Princeton University Press books are printed on acid-free paper and meet the guidelines for permanence and durability of the Committee on Production Guidelines for Book Longevity of the Council on Library Resources

Printed in the United States of America

10   9   8   7   6   5   4   3   2   1

10   9   8   7   6   5
(Pbk.)

The Lockert Library of Poetry in Translation is supported by a bequest from Charles Lacy Lockert (1888–1974)

# CONTENTS ❧

# ACKNOWLEDGMENTS 🐾

ACKNOWLEDGMENT is due to the editor of *The Irish Times*, where earlier versions of "Infinitive," "To Himself," and "To the Moon" appeared.

I have borrowed the epigraphs on page xxiv from versions by Ottavio Casale and Patrick Creagh, changing them a little here and there.

I would like to extend my grateful thanks to a few people who have contributed in one way or another to the evolution of these translations. To my teacher, the late Gioia Gaidoni, who first introduced me to Italian poetry; it has remained an unforgettable experience, and I remain always in her debt. To the late David Nolan, who was friend, teacher, and fellow enthusiast for the poems of Leopardi. To Rachel Kitzinger, who was there when I began these versions (in the garden of Michael and Ann Grant's house in Lucca), and has cheerfully suffered through more drafts of them than she or I would care to remember. To my friendly readers and advisors: Dana Gioia, George O'Brien, Lucia Amenta: to John Ahern of the Department of Italian, Vassar College, and to John F. Deane of Dedalus Press. Without their help and encouragement along the way, these versions of mine would be even more flawed than they are.

I would also like to thank Vassar College and the John Simon Guggenheim Foundation for the gift of time during which I was able to complete these translations.

# INTRODUCTION

# TO GIACOMO LEOPARDI

*John C. Barnes*

LEOPARDI was born in 1798, the eldest son of an aristocratic family with its seat in the small, backward provincial town of Recanati, near Ancona, which was then part of the Papal States. His mother was an austere, unfeeling woman with whom he appears to have had a minimal relationship, but his father, Count Monaldo, though reactionary, was himself a man of letters with a considerable private library, and made ample provision for his son's education in Latin, French, and Roman Catholic philosophy by the employment of clerical personal tutors. Giacomo was a child prodigy who by the age of fourteen had learned all his tutors could teach him and had already written his first literary compositions and works of scholarship. The next seven years were a period of "mad and desperate study" under his own direction in his father's library: he taught himself Greek, Hebrew, English, German, and Spanish, and embarked on philological studies by translating and annotating the classics. While his family expected him to pursue a career in the Church, he himself entertained academic ambitions, which were variously thwarted. Meanwhile, he had grown up an ugly, sickly young man with (like Joyce) precarious eyesight, but highly sensitive and incredibly learned, with an extraordinary memory. He was clearly one of those who have read "tous les livres."

Many of Leopardi's poems reveal his response to Recanati's beautiful landscape (indeed, apart from the slopes of Vesuvius this is the only landscape described in the *Canti*), but his relationship with his home town was a love-hate one: he regarded it as despicably provincial, and his father's palace as a suffocating prison, which he was unable to leave because his parents would not allow it—and they controlled the only purse to which he had access. Eventually, however, in November 1822, he was permitted to go to Rome as the guest of his mother's brother; but Rome was the capital of the backward Papal States and disappointed Leopardi as an intellectual and spiritual "desert" (a frequent metaphor for the aridity of life in his poetry), as well as confirming his ineptitude for social relationships. So after rather less than six months in Rome he returned to Recanati for another two years of tenacious work, one of the fruits of which was the first version of his *Operette morali*. In the summer of 1825, however, he accepted an invitation from his publisher, Antonio Fortunato Stella, to move to Milan to superintend an edition of the works of Cicero. Stella subsequently entrusted other projects to him, including a commentary on the poetry of Petrarch which remained the staple for the rest of the century. This work and private tuition supported him in Milan and, after a couple of months, in Bologna, which he found more congenial. But finally tiring of this directionless existence, Leopardi again returned to Recanati—though not for long because in 1827 he moved to Florence, where he was lionized by the liberal élite of the circle surrounding Giampiero Vieusseux, editor of the magazine *Antologia*. He wintered in Pisa but returned to Recanati in 1828. Two years later he accepted from his Tuscan friends an offer of financial support for another period in Florence, and left Recanati for the last time. During this second Florentine period he became a close friend of a Neapolitan exile, Antonio Ranieri. In 1833 he moved to Naples with Ranieri and Ranieri's sister, both of whom took devoted care of him during his declining years. In Naples he died in 1837, a few days short of his thirty-ninth birthday, and he is buried there.

Leopardi never married, indeed he was singularly luckless in his emotional attachments to women. His life was punctuated by three prominent cases of unrequited love, though it is often remarked that in the first two of them he was less concerned with love itself than with the idea of love. The first occurred in 1817 and involved his second cousin Countess Gertrude Cassi Lazzari, who had been married for nine years at the time. In Bologna in 1825 he was tormented by unreciprocated love for Countess Teresa Carniani Malvezzi. And Florence, between 1830 and 1833, was the scene of his last and greatest love, for Fanny Targioni Tozzetti, who was more interested in other suitors. This experience is reflected by five poems in the *Canti*, one of which is "To Himself." It is not generally suggested that the Silvia and the Nerina of the *Canti* represent cases of love.

Said by some critics to be Italy's second poet (after Dante), Leopardi is certainly (with Petrarch) one of her two greatest lyric poets. For the most part his poetry is intensely pessimistic in its view of the human condition. Three of its central motifs are those of hope, tedium, and pain—the pain arising from the realization that day-to-day existence is devoid of novelty and inspiration and that hope is merely an illusion. At first such pessimism is personal, but the atheist poet, seeing little purpose in life for mankind at large, gradually turns personal grief into cosmic melancholy and comes to see his own tragedy as only a minute part of the futile universal tragedy of human life. The amazing part of his tragic career is the uplifting quality of his verse. Even though logic convinces him of life's futility, the overall impression derived from reading most of his poems, particularly the idylls, is one of pleasure and joy. Emotionally and sentimentally, Leopardi is fully aware of the beauty of life around him; logically and philosophically, he sees that it is a waste of time to go on living. Nature is beautiful, but nature is a hidden force interested only in the perpetual destruction and regeneration of things and indifferent to whether humanity is happy or melancholic. Leopardi's search for a purpose in life led him deliberately to create great poetry, in which the love-hate relationship with nature and the inner struggle between logic and emotion are dominant themes. The *Canti* are his main collection of verse, which consists of thirty-four poems of varying lengths, composed between 1817 and 1837.

There is an element of genuine philosophy in Leopardi's thinking (indeed he has been seen as the greatest Italian thinker of his age), and at times this is one of the ingredients of the *Canti*, though his great moral and philosophical ideas are more fully expressed elsewhere: in brief fable form in his *Operette morali*;[1] in short, paragraphlike form (rather as Pascal's *Pensées*) in his *Pensieri*; and more extensively in parts of his vast "notebook" (*Zibaldone*), which also records his fertile ideas on poetry, society, philological questions, and psychological enquiries. These prose works are the natural complement to his poems.

Leopardi was eighteen when the Romantic *querelle* broke out in Italy with the publication of an article by Madame de Staël in the Milanese magazine *Biblioteca italiana*. At first Leopardi thought of himself as anti-Romantic, but by the time the earliest of the poems in the present volume was composed he had accepted—though very much on his own terms—that some aspects of Romanticism were not alien to him. Alfieri, Monti, and Foscolo were poets of immediately preceding generations who influenced some of his earlier poetry, particularly with the idea that literature has a social and political function. But it is with "Infinitive" that Leopardi fully discovers his own voice, setting aside public themes and

[1]Translated by Patrick Creagh as *Moral Tales* (Manchester: Carcanet New Press, 1983).

focusing on objects and landscapes which take on far-reaching emotional resonances. "Infinitive" is the first of a group of five poems composed between 1819 and 1821 (the first five in this selection), which Leopardi called "idylls." Here evocation and memory come to the fore, while grief at the dashing of cherished hopes and the inexorable passing of time is sublimated in calm contemplation of an immense, all-embracing nature. It was only later that Leopardi came to identify nature itself as the prime cause of human unhappiness, a view that underlies his "great idylls" of 1829–30 (from "The Solitary Thrush" to "Night Song of a Nomadic Shepherd in Asia"). These poems evince a sense of universal pain and a compassion that extends to all living people. The last poems, signally "Broom," fuse the motif of regret for hopes too soon destroyed with an ideological polemic against the facile optimism of moderate liberals attached to paltry ideas of progress. Resurrecting a strain of Titanism harking back to Enlightenment attitudes, he stresses the need for all to repudiate superficial consolatory myths and courageously to unite in brotherhood the better to confront the blind despotism of nature.

Very broadly speaking, it may be said that Italian literary Romanticism found its private voice in Leopardi and its public voice in Manzoni and his followers. Since questions of nationalism were as important as they were in Italy in the first half of the nineteenth century, Italian Romanticism was almost exclusively public-spirited, with the work of Leopardi as the only luminous exception. Thus Leopardi's influence in his own century was extremely limited: one might just about mention partial epigones such as Aleardo Aleardi and Giovanni Prati. Manzoni, in his own words, "failed to understand how Leopardi could pass as a poet" except in his early patriotic *canzoni*; Carducci dismissed him as monotonous, though Pascoli included him among the objects of his work as a critic. Fortunately, Italy's greatest literary critic of the century, Francesco De Sanctis, had a deep and lasting affinity with Leopardi, evinced in numerous studies published between 1849 and 1885. By the closing decades of the last century other kinds of influence were dominant, but the mark of Leopardi is nonetheless clear in certain later Italian poets, such as Pirandello, Cardarelli, Ungaretti, the early Saba, the early Quasimodo, and perhaps Montale; and Leopardi's prose and verse were usually cited as the examples to imitate by the influential literary magazine *La ronda*, directed by Cardarelli in the years around 1920. In one respect, though, many more poets have been indebted to Leopardi, since it was he who loosened the rigid metrical structure of the *canzone* and introduced freer lyric verse forms.

Greatness, however, is not to be measured in terms of influence; and Leopardi's greatness has long been assured. In the panorama of nineteenth-century poetry only Baudelaire is his rival.[2]

[2]I thank Jennifer Petrie for her comments on a preliminary draft of this introduction.

# TRANSLATOR'S INTRODUCTION ✌
## "ATTEMPTS AND PRELUDES"

I FIRST encountered Leopardi while studying Italian at University College, Dublin, in 1962. My enthusiasm was stimulated by a wonderful teacher of Italian poetry, Dr. Gioia Gaidoni, who simply walked us through the texts themselves, showing us how to care for and be responsible to the language, the images, the sentiments, the thoughts. She loved her poets, and what she communicated to us by example was something like that love, or at least a shadow of its possibility. Even though the B.A. marked the end of my formal study of Italian, Leopardi's poems have always remained in my mind as a clear, undiminished light. Their calm lucidity of understanding and expression, their combination of eloquence and idiomatic directness, created some subconscious notion of style for me, while their extremity of content—at once in touch with the cosmic and the quotidian; at once spiritually satisfying and intensely secular; at once personal to the point of solipsism and yet a powerful endorsement of human solidarity; full of romantic melancholy and nostalgia, yet bathed in the hard unflinching light of some sort of absolute courage in the face of existential despair (a mix we associated in the sixties with Camus, and part of which I later came to see in Beckett)—their extremity of content became a sort of benchmark for an unaided human and, in the best sense, materialist way of seeing.

Obviously I was not capable of emulating Leopardi in any of this. Still, the style and content of his poetry remained present and important to me, the image of a unique achievement—an achievement, I discovered, that was not readily apparent or persuasively available to the English-speaking world. There had been translations (a scholarly edition/translation of the complete poems, by G. L. Bickersteth appeared in 1923), but the most accomplished and satisfying of them, by John Heath-Stubbs, had been published in 1946, and was (and continues to be) out of print. A useful and sometimes successful collection by various translators, chief among them Muriel Kittel and Edwin Morgan, appeared in 1966 in America, edited by Angel Flores, and since then there have been translations by Arturo Vivante, Jean-Pierre Barricelli, some by Iris Origo in her good biography of the poet, and a selection by Ottavio Casale in his very useful

*Leopardi Reader*, which came out in 1981. In my opinion, however, none of these translations fully succeeded in bringing over the true feel and texture, the true sound of Leopardi into English (in the way, for example, Stephen Mitchell's versions of Rilke carry conviction for the English-speaking reader). This is not to say that my own version manages to do this, but only to suggest why I undertook the task in the first place, and stuck with it. And it is important to add that although I find all of the translations I have mentioned lacking in one way or another, I have in my own attempts many times learned from their solutions to our common problems: they have all at one point or another helped me to a closer understanding of what Leopardi might have "meant," and if their choices of English locutions seemed right and adequate, I did not deliberately seek out something different for the sake of difference, although my use of a similar solution might turn out looking not at all the same in the context of the whole poem. Translation must often be understood as a kind of cooperative effort, and one is always indebted to one's predecessors. (In fantasy, I often imagined the good job Coleridge might have done of translating Leopardi, the English poet's mixture of the lyrical and meditative manner, in pieces like "Frost at Midnight" or "This Lime Tree Bower My Prison," seeming most likely to capture something of Leopardi's voice and substance, and able—insofar as he was a contemporary, and therefore shared an idiom of expressive thought and feeling—to bring the Italian quickly into the bloodstream of English verse. At other times I'd expand this fantasy to a translation committee that included Coleridge, Wordsworth, Keats, Arnold, James Thomson—who translated some of Leopardi's prose and whose own poems show Leopardi's influence—Sam Johnson, Sam Beckett, and Wallace Stevens.)

My own beginning as a translator was modest. I first tried my hand at *L'Infinito*, dedicating that version to the memory of David Nolan, a friend and teacher, whose unhappily premature death in 1983 occurred while he was Professor of Italian at University College Dublin. After that, over the years, I began to work seriously, if piecemeal, on the poems gathered in this collection, discovering as I went along the difficulty, the impossibility, the essentially Leopardian nature of the task I had set myself, an enterprise that would always begin in the illusion of hope and move inexorably to the disillusion of the actual. (The image I found for it was that of the beautiful, brightly colored stone you see underwater, which, when you take home and set on a windowsill, turns out to be a dull, dead gray. The water—the element the colors live in—is the original language;

once removed from that, there is no finding those elemental colors again; we may only seek out approximations, painting them on as carefully as we can. Since this is a dual-language version, it will be very easy for the reader to see what I mean: on one page, the stone under water; on the other the dry, painted, "translated" stone.)

Still I persisted, driven by my regard for the originals and by my strong sense that Leopardi was the greatest European poet I knew who had not in any significant way entered into English-language literature and tradition. Mention the name Leopardi to ten educated people (poets included) in Ireland, England, America, or elsewhere in the English-speaking world, and it is likely that nine of them will shrug, knowing little or nothing about him or his poetry. But in his time Leopardi was a European star, and for the Italians he is still the most beloved of their poets, a poet without whom it would be impossible to think of modern Italian poetry as a whole, or of major figures such as Ungaretti, Montale, Quasimodo, Pavese.

Part of the problem, I suppose, is due to the changes of taste and fashion. Although the definition has to be carefully qualified, Leopardi was a Romantic. The Anglo-American poetic tradition in this century, however, has been essentially post-Romantic, an ironic subversion of many of the large emotional, philosophical, and rhetorical notes and gestures of the Romantics. And for all the chastity, classicism, and restrained intensity of his style, Leopardi's characteristic notes belong very much within this Romantic range, which (in English) can strike the contemporary Anglo-American-Irish ear as excessive, cloudy, artificially invocative, soft, sentimental, abstract or operatic.

Another problem in Leopardi's work itself may be the swiftness with which it changes gears from the lyrical to the philosophical, or from the evocative to the satirical: it can be at times, that is, a remarkably various, difficult, and unfamiliar medley of tones. Such shifts—which are often, even to Italians, a source of critical debate over the value of the work as a whole—are hard to convey convincingly in translation. So, even in the best of the English translations, Leopardi comes over in a somewhat *dated* way—his rhetoric (in English) often falling without emotional conviction on our ears: emotionally, intellectually, and rhetorically it can seem somewhat muscle-bound and self-regarding. The sheer speed, naturalness, and fluent transition we find in the Italian between eloquence and the most transparent plainness, between the quotidian and the grand, between lyrical evocation and philosophical demonstration, between thought and feeling, do not often come over into English with the same speed and pellucid ease as they possess in the Italian. And since these effects are of Leopardi's essence (tone is almost everything, and rhythm and musicality, and the lovely buoyancy of his lines and sentences), *he* does not come over in these translations as fully as I (in my innocence) thought he might, or as I was sure he needed to if we were to get something convincing about his stature and substance.

Thoughts like these were what fueled my ambition to do my own version. Of course the originals will always stand there as a painful reminder of the distance between ambition and achievement. (Once, on one of the few occasions I thought I was truly happy with my efforts, I discovered that this feeling of self-satisfaction was simply the result of my mistakenly reading the Italian poem and thinking, for a minute, that it was my English, that I had, at last, got it right.) But my aim, at least, was to touch something of the music, the rhythmic speed, the range, the fluency, the plangency—in a word, the feeling—of Leopardi's originals. In attempting this I have tried to be both faithful *and* interesting, seeing this double commitment as proper to the translator's art.

In more technical terms I would see my efforts as modeling themselves metrically, or at least rhythmically, on Leopardi's own supple freedom in his favored (but not exclusive) use of *versi sciolti*—hendecasyllabic blank verse—and *canzone libera*, a species of "organic form" free verse. I have not tried to follow him everywhere in his use of rhyme, since rhyming is so much more spontaneously available to the Italian language than it can be to many contemporary practitioners (including myself) of English verse. In texture of language itself I have sought a kind of idiomatic plainness that is never colloquial/contemporary, but that has about it a sort of straightforward and more or less timeless (that is, nonhistorically determined) feel. Simplicity and naturalness were qualities Leopardi himself most admired and aspired to, and I have felt that this is what I was trying to find in my own versions, while at the same time remaining faithful to some of those ways in which his expression, his idiom, is something foreign to our ears. In order to find a kind of equivalent to his music, without—as I have said—resorting to an exact following of his varying rhymes (which often remind me of how Milton operates in *Lycidas*), I have, as well as some casual rhyming, worked in a fair amount of assonantal play, something that comes naturally enough to me as someone writing out of an Irish literary context and tradition. Mostly, too, I have not done an exact line-by-line rendering; I have, however, tried to remain as close as possible to what I felt as the spirit of that equation, hoping that the English version would give some sense of the rhythmic evolution and poetic progression of lines to be found in the original.

The vagaries of translation are infinite: it all boils down to choices, to chosen solutions to essentially insoluble problems. What is asked of the responsible translator, I imagine, is a willingness to live a double life, to be committed in equal measure to two realities—the original poem, in its extraordinarily complex, integrated, and delicately orchestrated network of connections, and the poem the translator wants to write in his or her own language, which will be slowly pieced together until, with all its limitations, it possesses a life as equal to the whole life of the original as, for the moment, seems possible. In the end—as has been said about poems in general—a translation is "not finished but abandoned." To a French admirer who, in 1836, described him as *le poète de tous les hommes qui sentent*, Leopardi replied: *je n'ai jamais fait d'ouvrgae, j'ai fait seulement des essais en comptant toujours preluder*. Whatever about his own poems, it is surely the case that any translations of them can be no more than "attempts" and "preludes," which is how I would see the following versions (versions, I should add, which have already undergone some revisions for this American edition).

Finally, to speak of the Italian text itself, I have used various editions, mostly depending on the second edition of Mario Fubini's *Giacomo Leopardi: Canti, con Introduzione e Commento* (1971). My arrangement of the poems (fifteen of the thirty-six that are the complete *Canti*, plus "Coro dei Morti" from *Operette Morali*) is roughly chronological, and the three sections (not in the original, but which I thought might be helpful to the reader of the translations, allowing some pauses between poems) suggest, again roughly, those periods in Leopardi's life in which, for whatever complicated nexus of reasons, he wrote most of those poems for which he will—I am tempted, at the risk of his posthumous scorn, to say "always"—be remembered.

Since human existence itself is often felt to be irremediably dualistic, the task of translation, as I have described it above, may become (playfully or seriously) its own revealing metaphor for the divided nature of our lives. And while Leopardi does not seem to have made use of this metaphor, we do have his word for the hopelessness of the translator's task: *La perfetta poesia*, he says, *non è possibile a trasportarsi nelle lingue straniere*. Closer to home, I had the warning of the distinguished critic and scholar D. S. Carne-Ross to give me pause, who—in an essay on Leopardi a few years ago in *The New York Review of Books*—cautioned that "the translator of the *Canti* who suspects that his powers are not of this order [i.e. the order of the Milton of *Lycidas* and *Samson Agonistes,* or "the perfect gravity of Sophocles"] would do well to stick to plain prose." Infinite inferiority to Milton and Sophocles notwithstanding, I have turned my back on the scholar's advice, believing that it is only in verse, not "plain prose," that something of the true measure of Leopardi's achievement and greatness can be conveyed. My surviving hope is that there will be for every reader a few moments where, through the medium of my English, something of the pressure and presence of Leopardi's inimitable Italian voice may, however faintly, be heard.

*Not just individuals, but the whole human race always was and always will be unhappy by necessity. Not just the human race but all the animals. Not only the animals but all other beings in their own way. Not individuals only, but species, kinds, kingdoms, spheres, systems, worlds.*

(Zibaldone, 4175)

*Works of [literary] genius have this intrinsic quality, that even when they capture exactly the nothingness of things, or vividly reveal and make us feel life's inevitable unhappiness, or express the most acute hopelessness . . . they are always a source of consolation and renewed enthusiasm, even if they have no other subject but death, giving their reader back—at least for a little while—the life he has lost. . . . Indeed, the spectacle of nothingness presented by such works actually seems to enlarge the soul of the reader, to lift it up and reconcile it to its own despair.*

(Zibaldone, 259–60)

*Everyone wants to write poetry, but prefers reading prose. And you know well this century is not and cannot be poetic. A poet, even a great one, attracts little attention, and even if he gains fame in his own country, it is hard for his reputation to spread to the rest of Europe, because perfect poetry cannot be carried over into foreign languages, and because Europe wants something more solid and more real than poetry.*

(Leopardi, letter to Francesco Puccinotti, June 5, 1826)

# ❦ ONE ❦

# L'INFINITO 🐾

Sempre caro mi fu quest'ermo colle,
E questa siepe, che da tanta parte
Dell'ultimo orizzonte il guardo esclude.
Ma, sedendo e mirando, interminati
5    Spazi di là da quella, e sovrumani
Silenzi, e profondissima quiete
Io nel pensier mi fingo; ove per poco
Il cor non si spaura. E come il vento
Odo stormir tra queste piante, io quello
10   Infinito silenzio a questa voce
Vo comparando: e mi sovvien l'eterno,
E le morte stagioni, e la presente
E viva, e il suon di lei. Così tra questa
Immensità s'annega il pensier mio;
15   E il naufragar m'è dolce in questo mare.

1819

## INFINITIVE

I've always loved this lonesome hill
And this hedge that hides
The entire horizon, almost, from sight.
But sitting here in a daydream, I picture
The boundless spaces away out there, silences
Deeper than human silence, an unfathomable hush
In which my heart is hardly a beat
From fear. And hearing the wind
Rush rustling through these bushes,
I pit its speech against infinite silence—
And a notion of eternity floats to mind,
And the dead seasons, and the season
Beating here and now, and the sound of it. So,
In this immensity my thoughts all drown;
And it's easeful to be wrecked in seas like these.

# LA SERA DEL DI' DI FESTA

Dolce e chiara è la notte e senza vento,
E queta sovra i tetti e in mezzo agli orti
Posa la luna, e di lontan rivela
Serena ogni montagna. O donna mia,
Già tace ogni sentiero, e pei balconi
Rara traluce la notturna lampa:
Tu dormi, che t'accolse agevol sonno
Nelle tue chete stanze; e non ti morde
Cura nessuna; e già non sai né pensi
Quanta piaga m'apristi in mezzo al petto.
Tu dormi: io questo ciel, che sì benigno
Appare in vista, a salutar m'affaccio,
E l'antica natura onnipossente,
Che mi fece all'affanno. — A te la speme
Nego — mi disse, — anche la speme; e d'altro
Non brillin gli occhi tuoi se non di pianto. —
Questo dì fu solenne: or da' trastulli
Prendi riposo; e forse ti rimembra
In sogno a quanti oggi piacesti, e quanti
Piacquero a te: non io, non già ch'io speri,
Al pensier ti ricorro. Intanto io chieggo
Quanto a viver mi resti, e qui per terra
Mi getto, e grido, e fremo. O giorni orrendi
In così verde etate! Ahi! per la via
Odo non lunge il solitario canto
Dell' artigian, che riede a tarda notte,
Dopo i sollazzi, al suo povero ostello;
E fieramente mi si stringe il core,
A pensar come tutto al mondo passa,
E quasi orma non lascia. Ecco è fuggito
Il dì festivo, ed al festivo il giorno

# SUNDAY EVENING

The night bright and easy, not a breath
Of wind: calmly the moon hangs
Above the rooftops and kitchen gardens,
Revealing in the distance the clear
Outline of every mountain. Now, my dear,
The narrow streets are still, only a few
Last shutters are barred with lamplight:
Taken easily by sleep, you lie
Untroubled in your hushed rooms,
Without a thought for the wound
You've opened in my heart.
You sleep, while I say goodnight
To the kindly-seeming sky
And to nature—ancient, all-powerful—
Who shaped me for suffering. —*To you,*
She said, *I refuse even hope; your eyes*
*Will shine with nothing but tears.*
Today was a holiday, and now
You rest from your games, remembering
In a dream, perhaps, how many men
You pleased, how many pleased you:
I am not, nor could I hope to be,
Among your thoughts. And so
Wondering how long I have left to live,
I sink down, cry out, my whole body
Trembling. Such black, black days
In so green a season! And ah, now
On the street outside I can hear
The lonesome song a workman sings
On his midnight way home from the inn
To his poor cottage, and sorely
My heart is shaken at the thought
Of how everything in the world goes by
And leaves so little trace behind. Look
How this feast-day is over in a flash,

Volgar succede, e se ne porta il tempo
Ogni umano accidente. Or dov'è il suono
Di que' popoli antichi? or dov'è il grido
35   De' nostri avi famosi, e il grande impero
Di quella Roma, e l'armi, e il fragorío
Che n'andò per la terra e l'oceano?
Tutto è pace e silenzio, e tutto posa
Il mondo, e più di lor non si ragiona.
40   Nella mia prima età, quando s'aspetta
Bramosamente il dì festivo, or poscia
Ch'egli era spento, io doloroso, in veglia,
Premea le piume; ed alla tarda notte
Un canto che s'udia per li sentieri
45   Lontanando morire a poco a poco,
Già similmente mi stringeva il core.

1820

The work-day comes on, and time takes away
All we are and do. Now
Where are all the ancient voices? who
Now hears the clamor and far-flung stir
Our famous ancestors made in the world?
And where is Rome's own empire now
And her armies, whose clanging din
Once rang over land and sea? All
Is peace, all quiet, the whole world still,
And they are spoken of no more.
When I was a child, I used to wait
In a fever of desire for Sunday,
And when it was over I'd lie awake
Brokenhearted, sobbing to my pillow;
And then, in the small hours, a song
I'd hear dying away little by little
Through the back streets of town
Would make my heart ache as it's aching now.

# ALLA LUNA 🐝

O graziosa luna, io mi rammento
Che, or volge l'anno, sovra questo colle
Io venia pien d'angoscia a rimirarti:
E tu pendevi allor su quella selva,
    5    Siccome or fai, che tutta la rischiari.
Ma nebuloso e tremulo dal pianto,
Che mi sorgea sul ciglio, alle mie luci
Il tuo volto apparia, che travagliosa
Era mia vita: ed è, né cangia stile,
   10   O mia diletta luna. E pur mi giova
La ricordanza, e il noverar l'etate
Del mio dolore. Oh come grato occorre
Nel tempo giovanil, quando ancor lungo
La speme e breve ha la memoria il corso,
   15   Il rimembrar delle passate cose,
Ancor che triste, e che l'affanno duri!

1819

## TO THE MOON

Now that the year has come full circle,
I remember climbing this hill, heartbroken,
To gaze up at the graceful sight of you,
And how you hung then above those woods
As you do tonight, bathing them in brightness.
But at that time your face seemed nothing
But a cloudy shimmering through my tears,
So wretched was the life I led: and lead still . . .
Nothing changes, moon of my delight. Yet
I find pleasure in recollection, in calling back
My season of grief: when one is young,
And hope is a long road, memory
A short one, how welcome then
The remembrance of things past—no matter
How sad, and the heart still grieving.

# IL SOGNO

Era il mattino, e tra le chiuse imposte
Per lo balcone insinuava il sole
Nella mia cieca stanza il primo albore;
Quando, in sul tempo che più leve il sonno
5  E più soave le pupille adombra,
Stettemi allato e riguardommi in viso
Il simulacro di colei che amore
Prima insegnommi, e poi lasciommi in pianto.
Morta non mi parea, ma trista, e quale
10  Degl'infelici è la sembianza. Al capo
Appressommi la destra, e sospirando,
— Vivi — mi disse — e ricordanza alcuna
Serbi di noi? — Donde — risposi — e come
Vieni, o cara beltà? Quanto, deh! quanto
15  Di te mi dolse e duol: né mi credea
Che risaper tu lo dovessi; e questo
Facea più sconsolato il dolor mio.
Ma sei tu per lasciarmi un'altra volta?
Io n'ho gran tema. Or dimmi, e che t'avvenne?
20  Sei tu quella di prima? E que ti strugge
Internamente? — Obblivione ingombra
I tuoi pensieri, e gli avviluppa il sonno,
Disse colei. — Son morta, e mi vedesti
L'ultima volta, or son più lune. — Immensa
25  Doglia m'oppresse a queste voci il petto.
Ella seguì: — Nel fior degli anni estinta,
Quand'è il viver più dolce, e pria che il core
Certo si renda com'è tutta indarno
L'umana speme. A desiar colei,
30  Che d'ogni affanno il tragge, ha poco andare
L'egro mortal; ma sconsolata arriva
La morte ai giovanetti, e duro è il fato
Di quella speme che sotterra è spenta.
Vano è saper quel che natura asconde

# DREAM 🖋

It was morning, and through tight shutters
The first faint glimmer of sunlight slipped
Into my darkened bedroom. At that hour
When sleep, it seems, weighs next to nothing,
Lays barely a shadow along one's eyes,
I saw at my bedside, staring down,
The girl who first taught me what love is
And then left me grieving. She didn't
Seem dead, but downcast, like a lost soul.
Laying her hand on my head, she sighed
And said, —Are you still alive? Do you
Remember me at all? —Light of my life,
I answered, where have you come from?
How did you get here? I grieved for you so,
And go on grieving; and believing
You couldn't know, I grieved the more.
But are you going to leave me again?
I tremble even at the thought. Tell me
What happened. Are you as you were?
What is it torments you? —Forgetfulness
And sleep, she said, have set your wits astray.
Indeed I'm dead, and months have gone by
Since last you saw me. Hearing these words,
My heart turned to stone. And she went on:
—I died early, when life is sweet, before
One knows all human hope is vain.
It doesn't take long for mortal misery
To learn to call upon death itself
As its sovereign cure; but there can be
No consolation when children die,
And nothing could know a crueler fate
Than that hope buried in an early grave.
It isn't any good for the innocent young
To see into nature's hidden secrets,

35    Agl'inesperti della vita, e molto
All'immatura sapienza il cieco
Dolor prevale. — Oh sfortunata, oh cara,
Taci, taci — diss'io, — chè tu mi schianti
Con questi detti il cor. Dunque sei morta,
40    O mia diletta, ed io son vivo, ed era
Pur fisso in ciel che quei sudori estremi
Cotesta cara e tenerella salma
Provar dovesse, a me restasse intera
Questa misera spoglia? Oh quante volte,
45    In ripensar che più non vivi, e mai
Non avverrà ch'io ti ritrovi al mondo,
Creder nol posso. Ahi ahi, che cosa è questa
Che morte s'addimanda? Oggi per prova
Intenderlo potessi, e il capo inerme
50    Agli atroci del fato odii sottrarre!
Giovane son, ma si consuma e perde
La giovanezza mia come vecchiezza;
La qual pavento, e pur m'è lunge assai.
Ma poco da vecchiezza si discorda
55    Il fior dell'età mia. — Nascemmo al pianto—
Disse — ambedue; felicità non rise
Al viver nostro; e dilettossi il cielo
De' nostri affanni. — Or, se di pianto il ciglio—
Soggiunsi — e di pallor velato il viso
60    Per la tua dipartita, e se d'angoscia
Porto gravido il cor; dimmi: d'amore
Favilla alcuna, o di pietà, giammai
Verso il misero amante il cor t'assalse
Mentre vivesti? Io disperando allora
65    E sperando traea le notti e i giorni;
Oggi nel vano dubitar si stanca
La mente mia. Che se una volta sola
Dolor ti strinse di mia negra vita,
Non mel celar, ti prego, e mi soccorra
70    La rimembranza or che il futuro è tolto
Ai nostri giorni. E quella: — Ti conforta,
O sventurato. Io di pietade avara
Non ti fui, mentre vissi, ed or non sono,

And random suffering cancels all
Such raw, unripened knowledge. —Hush,
I said, my poor dear, hush. These words of yours
Are breaking my heart. So you're dead, my darling,
And I'm alive. Was it heaven's will
That your warm, cherished flesh should feel
The sweat of death, while my worthless bones
Remained unscathed? How often
When I thought of you dead, and thought
I'd never see you again in the world,
I couldn't believe it. But, alas, what is
This thing called death? It seems, if ever,
I should be able this day to say for sure, and so
Guard this helpless self against heartless stars.
I'm young yet, but my youth is a withering
Just like age, which I'm afraid of,
Far off as it is. And in plain truth
There's no great difference to be seen
Between old age and these green days.
—Both of us, she said, were born to suffer:
Our lives lacked joy, and the heavens took
Pleasure in our pain. —If ever I wept,
I said, or grew pale for your going,
And if I bear this weight of woe in my heart,
Then tell me: did even the smallest spark
Of love or pity ever touch your breast
For your wretched lover? I, night and day,
Had to dangle between hope and despair,
And doubt still plagues me. If, just once,
You felt the slightest pang for this
Misbegotten life of mine, I beg you
Not hide it from me, since that memory
Could be some comfort now, now
Our future's been wiped away. At this
She said, —Be comforted, unhappy man:
I was not without pity while I lived,
Nor am I now; I also was unhappy;

Che fui misera anch'io. Non far querela
75 Di questa infelicissima fanciulla.
Per le sventure nostre, e per l'amore
Che mi strugge — esclamai, — per lo diletto
Nome di giovanezza e la perduta
Speme dei nostri dì, concedi, o cara,
80 Che la tua destra io tocchi. Ed ella, in atto
Soave e tristo, la porgeva. Or mentre
Di baci la ricopro e d'affannosa
Dolcezza palpitando all'anelante
Seno la stringo, di sudore il volto
85 Ferveva e il petto, nelle fauci stava
La voce, al guardo traballava il giorno.
Quando colei teneramente affissi
Gli occhi negli occhi miei: — Già scordi, o caro
Disse, — che di beltà son fatta ignuda,
90 E tu d'amore, o sfortunato, indarno
Ti scaldi e fremi? Or finalmente addio.
Nostre misere menti e nostre salme
Son disgiunte in eterno. A me non vivi
E mai più non vivrai: già ruppe il fato
95 La fé che mi giurasti. Allor, d'angoscia
Gridar volendo, e spasimando, e pregne
Di sconsolato pianto le pupille,
Dal sonno mi disciolsi. Ella negli occhi
Pur mi restava, e nell'incerto raggio
100 Del sol vederla io mi credeva ancora.

1821

Don't grieve for this woebegone girl.
Then I cried out, —By our crossed fortunes
And the love that destroys me; in the dear
Name of youth and the dead hope
Of the days we shared, let me, my love,
Let me touch your hand. And she,
With a gesture both gentle and sad,
Gave me her hand. Then,
While I cover it in kisses and press it hard
With bittersweet tremblings to my pounding heart,
My face and breast were scalding with sweat,
My voice was choking in my throat, daylight
Was wavering before my gaze. Tenderly, then,
She fixed her eyes in mine and said,
—My dear, have you forgotten so soon
I've been stripped of beauty? Poor thing,
You shiver and burn with love in vain.
Now, one final time, farewell.
Our bodies and our wretched minds
Are severed forever. You cannot
Live for me now, nor evermore: fate
Has broken already those vows you made.
At this, wanting to shriek aloud in pain
And shuddering from head to foot,
My eyes swollen with hopeless tears,
I wrenched myself from sleep. Still
She stood there before my gaze, and
In the sun's first faint shimmering light
I would have sworn I could see her still.

# LA VITA SOLITARIA ✸

La mattutina pioggia, allor che l'ale
Battendo esulta nella chiusa stanza
La gallinella, ed al balcon s'affaccia
L'abitator de' campi, e il sol che nasce
5    I suoi tremuli rai fra le cadenti
Stille saetta, alla capanna mia
Dolcemente picchiando, mi risveglia;
E sorgo, e i lievi nugoletti, e il primo
Degli augelli susurro, e l'aura fresca,
10    E le ridenti piagge benedico:
Poiché voi, cittadine infauste mura,
Vidi e conobbi assai, là dove segue
Odio al dolor compagno; e doloroso
Io vivo, e tal morrò, deh tosto! Alcuna
15    Benché scarsa pietà pur mi dimostra
Natura in questi lochi, un giorno oh quanto
Verso me più cortese! E tu pur volgi
Dai miseri lo sguardo; e tu, sdegnando
Le sciagure e gli affanni, alla reina
20    Felicità servi, o Natura. In cielo,
In terra amico agl'infelici alcuno
E rifugio non resta altro che il ferro.

Talor m'assido in solitaria parte,
Sovra un rialto, al margine d'un lago
25    Di taciturne piante incoronato.
Ivi, quando il meriggio in ciel si volve,
La sua tranquilla imago il sol dipinge,
Ed erba o foglia non si crolla al vento;
E non onda incresparsi, e non cicala
30    Strider, né batter penna augello in ramo,
Né farfalla ronzar, né voce o moto
Da presso né da lunge odi né vedi.
Tien quelle rive altissima quiete;

# THE LIFE OF SOLITUDE 🦎

Ticking lightly on my cabin roof,
The morning rain wakes me: the hens
Are flapping at the walls of their coop,
The farmer stands looking out from his porch,
And the rays of the rising sun
Shimmer with raindrops. Getting up,
I bless the little wisps of cloud
And the early birds' first murmurings
And the fresh breeze and brightening hills—
For I've seen enough of wretched cities
Where hatred dogs unhappiness, and where
I live in misery and will, soon enough,
In misery die. Here nature still lends me
At least a little compassion—who once
Was full of kindness and real comfort.
For even you, Nature, will turn away
From the wretched of the earth; even you,
Scorning calamities and crosses, smile
Only on those who lead happy lives.
In heaven, on earth, the lost ones
Can find neither friend nor refuge
Except in their own cold steel.

Sometimes I sit in a deserted spot
On a bank at the edge of a lake
Bordered by trees that make no sound.
There, in the middle of the afternoon,
The sun casts its still reflection on water,
And not a breath of wind stirs a single leaf
Or a single blade of grass, and you can't
See or hear, near or far, a ripple of water
Nor a cricket chirping, nor a wingbeat
Flittering in leaves, nor an insect buzzing,
Nor any sound or any movement at all.
A profound hush settles, and sitting quite still

17

Ond'io quasi me stesso e il mondo obblio
35 Sedendo immoto; e già mi par che sciolte
Giaccian le membra mie, né spirto o senso
Più le commova, e lor quiete antica
Co' silenzi del loco si confonda.

Amore, amore, assai lungi volasti
40 Dal petto mio, che fu sì caldo un giorno,
Anzi rovente. Con sua fredda mano
Lo strinse la sciaura, e in ghiaccio è vòlto
Nel fior degli anni. Mi sovvien del tempo
Che mi scendesti in seno. Era quel dolce
45 E irrevocabil tempo, allor che s'apre
Al guardo giovanil questa infelice
Scena del mondo, e gli sorride in vista
Di paradiso. Al garzoncello il core
Di vergine speranza e di desio
50 Balza nel petto; e già s'accinge all'opra
Di questa vita, come a danza o gioco,
Il misero mortal. Ma non sì tosto,
Amor, di te m'accorsi, e il viver mio
Fortuna avea già rotto, ed a questi occhi
55 Non altro convenia che il pianger sempre.
Pur, se talvolta per le piagge apriche,
Su la tacita aurora o quando al sole
Brillano i tetti e i poggi e le campagne,
Scontro di vaga donzelletta il viso;
60 O qualor nella placida quiete
D'estiva notte, il vagabondo passo
Di rincontro alle ville soffermando,
L'erma terra contemplo, e di fanciulla,
Che all'opre di sua man la notte aggiunge,
65 Odo sonar nelle romite stanze
L'arguto canto; a palpitar si move
Questo mio cor di sasso: ahi, ma ritorna
Tosto al ferreo sopor, ch'è fatto estrano
Ogni moto soave al petto mio.

I almost forget myself and the world:
My body seems to melt away and my limbs
Seem drained of spirit and motion, their ancient calm
Dissolving into that deep silence.

Love, love, how far you have flown
Away from this heart, which burned once
Even to distraction. Frostbitten by sorrow,
It froze in the bud. I can remember
The day you first came to me. It was
That sweet unrepeatable season
When the sad stage of this world seems
To young eyes a paradise of smiles:
In its very first virgin flush of hope
A boy's heart gallops with desire
As he, hapless poor creature that he is,
Plunges into the business of living
As if it were only a game or a dance.
But as soon, love, as I met you,
Misfortune wrecked my life and left me
In mourning forever. And yet there are
Still times among these open spaces—
In the wide silence around dawn
Or when roofs and meadows and little hills
Are shining in the sun—when I catch
A glimpse of a pretty face; or times
In the stillness of a summer night,
Strolling among the country houses
And stopping to brood on the world
Lonesome all round me, when I hear
Echoing through deserted rooms
The clear sweet song of a girl
Who works, weaving, late into the night;
And then this heart of stone may start
Beating faster: but, alas, how quickly
It will sink back into its leaden sleep—
Since every tender feeling by now
Has become, to me, a total stranger.

70     O cara luna, al cui tranquillo raggio
        Danzan le lepri nelle selve; e duolsi
        Alla mattina il cacciator, che trova
        L'orme intricate e false, e dai covili
        Error vario lo svia; salve, o benigna
75     Delle notti reina. Infesto scende
        Il raggio tuo fra macchie e balze o dentro
        A deserti edifici, in su l'acciaro
        Del pallido ladron ch'a teso orecchio
        Il fragor delle rote e de' cavalli
80     Da lungi osserva o il calpestio de' piedi
        Sulla tacita via; poscia improvviso
        Col suon dell'armi e con la rauca voce
        E col funereo ceffo il core agghiaccia
        Al passegger, cui semivivo e nudo
85     Lascia in breve tra' sassi. Infesto occorre
        Per le contrade cittadine il bianco
        Tuo lume al drudo vil, che degli alberghi
        Va radendo le mura e la secreta
        Ombra seguendo, e resta, e si spaura
90     Delle ardenti lucerne e degli aperti
        Balconi. Infesto alle malvage menti,
        A me sempre benigno il tuo cospetto
        Sarà per queste piagge, ove non altro
        Che lieti colli e spaziosi campi
95     M'apri alla vista. Ed ancor io soleva,
        Bench'innocente io fossi, il tuo vezzoso
        Raggio accusar negli abitati lochi,
        Quand'ei m'offriva al guardo umano, e quando
        Scopriva umani aspetti al guardo mio.
100    Or sempre loderollo, o ch'io ti miri
        Veleggiar tra le nubi, o che serena
        Dominatrice dell'etereo campo,
        Questa flebil riguardi umana sede.
        Me spesso rivedrai solingo e muto
105    Errar pe' boschi e per le verdi rive,
        O seder sovra l'erbe, assai contento
        Se core e lena a sospirar m'avanza.

1821

Beloved moon, mild queen of night,
By whose peaceful light the hares
Make game among the trees, their crazy tracks
Baffling the hunter who comes at dawn
And follows them farther and farther from their lair.
This light of yours isn't welcome at all
Among crags and thickets and buildings
Abandoned to the night, where the knife
Of the white-faced highwayman glints
As he listens for distant wheels and horses
Or the crunch of footsteps on the silent road:
With a sudden sword-rattle, hoarse shouts,
And the terrible look of death itself,
He'll freeze the traveler in his tracks
And in no time at all leave him there
Half dead, stark naked, among the stones.
Unwelcome, too, is your pale light
To city streets where the lecher skulks
By gable walls or lurks in shadow
And moves by fits and starts, afraid
Of the bright lights and open windows. Hateful
To all such minds of malice, the sight of you
Will always be a blessing to me here
Where my eyes meet nothing but broad fields
And cheerful hills. Once, in my innocence,
Even I used hate your glimmering light
When it shone where people haunted—
Exposing me to human looks, or forcing
Me to see human faces. But now I am
All praise, whether I glimpse your misty image
Among the clouds, or whether—reigning
In silent majesty over the fields of heaven—
You gaze down on this mortal world
Of weeping voices. Me you will often find
Wandering alone and silent through the woods
And along these green banks, or just
Lying in the grass, happy enough if I
Have heart and breath left to breathe a sigh.

# ULTIMO CANTO DI SAFFO

Placida notte, e verecondo raggio
Della cadente luna; e tu che spunti
Fra la tacita selva in su la rupe,
Nunzio del giorno; oh dilettose e care,
5    Mentre ignote mi fûr l'erinni e il fato,
Sembianze agli occhi miei; già non arride
Spettacol molle ai disperati affetti.
Noi l'insueto allor gaudio ravviva,
Quando per l'etra liquido si volve
10   E per li campi trepidanti il flutto
Polveroso de' Noti, e quando il carro,
Grave carro di Giove, a noi sul capo
Tonando, il tenebroso aere divide.
Noi per le balze e le profonde valli
15   Natar giova tra' nembi, e noi la vasta
Fuga de' greggi sbigottiti, o d'alto
Fiume alla dubbia sponda
Il suono e la vittrice ira dell'onda.

Bello il tuo manto, o divo cielo, e bella
20   Sei tu, rorida terra. Ahi di cotesta
Infinita beltà parte nessuna
Alla misera Saffo i numi e l'empia
Sorte non fenno. A' tuoi superbi regni
Vile, o Natura, e grave ospite addetta,
25   E dispregiata amante, alle vezzose
Tue forme il core e le pupille invano
Supplichevole intendo. A me non ride
L'aprico margo, e dall'eterea porta
Il mattutino albor; me non il canto
30   De' colorati augelli, e non de' faggi
Il murmure saluta; e dove all'ombra
Degl'inchinati salici dispiega
Candido rivo il puro seno, al mio
Lubrico piè le flessuose linfe
35   Disdegnando sottragge,
E preme in fuga l'odorate spiagge.

# SAPPHO'S LAST SONG  ✑

Peaceful night, shamefaced light
Of the fading moon, and you, star of the morning,
As you rise above silent cliff-top woods—
How I loved fine sights like these
Before learning what fate and the Furies were;
But such calm, quiet scenes can now
Cheer my hopeless heart no more.
I feel, now, such unaccustomed joy
Only when dusty southern winds
Cleave the clear air and swirl a path
Through shivering grass, or thunder rolls
Like Jove's great chariot over my head,
Splitting the pitch-black air wide open. Now
It is stormy weather I love plunging into
Along the crags and through deep valleys,
Seeing terror-stricken flocks in scattered flight,
Or hearing wave after wave go rushing over
Crumbled banks: the swollen torrent's headlong roar.

How gorgeous the earth is, drenched in dew,
And your wide cloak, divine sky. But ah,
The gods and grim-lipped fate have given
Poor Sappho no part of this infinite beauty.
A tiresome wretched guest in your
Grand, indifferent domain, Nature,
I lift like an abandoned lover
My beggar's heart and beggar's eyes
Up to all your lovely forms. The sunny
Riverbanks don't smile at me, nor dawn's
White light in the sky; bright-winged birds
Don't sing to me, beechtrees don't greet me
With murmuring leaves, and where clear water
Runs under the bending willow's shade
The stream slides and winds away
In scorn from these soiled and slippery feet,
Hugging the sweet-scented bank as it flees.

Qual fallo mai, qual sì nefando eccesso
Macchiommi anzi il natale, onde sì torvo
Il ciel mi fosse e di fortuna il volto?
40 In che peccai bambina, allor che ignara
Di misfatto è la vita, onde poi scemo
Di giovanezza, e disfiorato, al fuso
Dell'indomita Parca si volvesse
Il ferrigno mio stame? Incaute voci
45 Spande il tuo labbro: i destinati eventi
Move arcano consiglio. Arcano è tutto,
Fuor che il nostro dolor. Negletta prole
Nascemmo al pianto, e la ragione in grembo
De' celesti si posa. Oh cure, oh speme
50 De' più verd' anni! Alle sembianze il Padre,
Alle amene sembianze eterno regno
Diè nelle genti; e per virili imprese,
Per dotta lira o canto,
Virtù non luce in disadorno ammanto.

55 Morremo. Il velo indegno a terra sparto,
Rifuggirà l'ignudo animo a Dite,
E il crudo fallo emenderà del cieco
Dispensator de' casi. E tu cui lungo
Amore indarno, e lunga fede, e vano
60 D'implacato desio furor mi strinse,
Vivi felice, se felice in terra
Visse nato mortal. Me non asperse
Del soave licor del doglio avaro
Giove, poi che perir gl'inganni e il sogno
65 Della mia fanciullezza. Ogni più lieto
Giorno di nostra età primo s'invola.
Sottentra il morbo, e la vecchiezza, e l'ombra
Della gelida morte. Ecco di tante
Sperate palme e dilettosi errori,
70 Il Tartaro m'avanza; e il prode ingegno
Han la tenaria Diva,
E l'atra notte, e la silente riva.

1822

What offense, what loathsome crime marked me
Before I was born, making heaven and the face
Of fortune frown as they did? What sin
Did I commit as a child—when one can know
No wrong at all—that my iron-dark thread of life,
Lacking all the summer colors of youth,
Lay twisted on fate's implacable spindle? Reckless
Words fly from your mouth: *A hidden purpose*
*Fashions whatever has to happen. Everything is hidden*
*Except our pain. We come, a forsaken race,*
*Crying into the world, and the gods*
*Keep their own counsel.* Ah, those hopes and cares
Of our early years! God gives to good looks
Lasting power amongst men and women:
Neither high heroic deeds nor skill
In lyric song or learned poem will shine
Through the tattered coat of a body like mine.

I shall die. With its poor unworthy cloak cast off,
My naked soul will seek some refuge
In the land of the dead, righting the cruel wrong
That chance—blindly parceling out our lives—
Inflicted. And you for whom I've spent the years
In fruitless love—faithful forever, forever burning
In an empty frenzy of unsatisfied desire—
Be happy, if any mortal at all on earth
May be happy. From his miser's store
Of sweet blessings, God gave me nothing
Once my dream of youth and its illusions
Withered. Our happiest days are first to fly,
Leaving illness, old age, and the icy-handed
Shadow of death. And so, of all those hopes
And high ambitions, all those dear
Enchantments of the heart, only death itself
Is left; and this quick, bright spirit of mine
To the queen of shadows must be handed over,
And to black night, and the speechless shore.

# CORO DEI MORTI &#x25A8;

Sola nel mondo eterna, a cui si volve
Ogni creata cosa,
In te, morte, si posa
Nostra ignuda natura;
5     Lieta no, ma sicura
Dall' antico dolor. Profonda notte
Nella confusa mente
Il pensier grave oscura;
Alla speme, al desio, l'arido spirito
10    Lena mancar si sente:
Così d'affanno e di temenza è sciolto,
E l'età vote e lente
Senza tedio consuma.

Vivemmo: e qual di paurosa larva,
15    E di sudato sogno,
A lattante fanciullo erra nell'alma
Confusa ricordanza:
Tal memoria n'avanza
Del viver nostro; ma da tema è lunge
20    Il rimembrar. Che fummo?
Che fu quel punto acerbo
Che di vita ebbe nome?
Cosa arcana e stupenda
Oggi è la vita al pensier nostro, e tale
25    Qual de' vivi al pensiero
L'ignota morte appar. Come da morte
Vivendo rifuggia, così rifugge
Dalla fiamma vitale
Nostra ignuda natura;
30    Lieta no ma sicura,
Però ch'esser beato
Nega ai mortali e nega a' morti il fato.

1824

# CHORUS OF THE DEAD

Only immortal in the world,
Terminus of all things living,
Our nature—naked as it is—
Comes, Death, to rest in you;
Happy, no, but safe
From that sorrow
Old as time. Deep night keeps
The dark thought of you
From the rambling mind;
Spent, the spirit feels
Its springs of hope and of desire
Dry up: fears and sorrows slip away
And it passes with no pain
Through the long slow vacant
Ages of eternity.

Once we were alive:
As the infant at the breast
Remembers in a kind of mist
Its spectral frights and nightsweats,
We remember, but free from fear,
Our own lives. What were we?
What was that bitter instant
We called life? Life to us now
Seems a strange astonishment,
As death, all unknown,
Seems mysterious to the living.
And as in life our naked
Unaccommodated nature
Sought shelter from death,
So now it flies life's quickening flame:
Happy, no, but safe—since fate
Forbids the state of bliss
Both to the living and the dead.

# ❧ TWO ❧

# A SILVIA

Silvia, rimembri ancora
Quel tempo della tua vita mortale,
Quando beltà splendea
Negli occhi tuoi ridenti e fuggitivi,
E tu, lieta e pensosa, il limitare
Di gioventù salivi?

Sonavan le quiete
Stanze, e le vie dintorno,
Al tuo perpetuo canto,
Allor che all'opre femminili intenta
Sedevi, assai contenta
Di quel vago avvenir che in mente avevi.
Era il maggio odoroso: e tu solevi
Così menare il giorno.

Io, gli studi leggiadri
Talor lasciando e le sudate carte,
Ove il tempo mio primo
E di me si spendea la miglior parte,
D' in su i veroni del paterno ostello
Porgea gli orecchi al suon della tua voce,
Ed alla man veloce
Che percorrea la faticosa tela.
Mirava il ciel sereno,
Le vie dorate e gli orti,
E quinci il mar da lungi, e quindi il monte.
Lingua mortal non dice
Quel ch'io sentiva in seno.

Che pensieri soavi,
Che speranze, che cori, o Silvia mia!
Quale allor ci apparia
La vita umana e il fato!

## TO SILVIA

Silvia, do you still remember
The time in your brief life here
When beauty brightened
Your eyes and your shy smile,
And you stood in pensive joy on the brink
Of becoming a young woman?

All day the hushed rooms
And the roads around the house
Rang with your singing
As you bent to the spinning wheel,
Happily adrift in your hazy
Dreams of the future. Day
After day you spent like that,
All the fragrant month of May.

Sometimes, getting up
From the books I loved
And those sweat-stained pages
Where I spent the best of my youth,
I'd lean from the terrace of my father's house
Toward the sound of your voice
And the quick click of your hands
At the heavy loom. Wonder-struck, I'd stare
Up at the cloudless blue of the sky,
Out at the kitchen gardens and the roads
That shone like gold, and off there
To the mountains and, there, to the distant sea.
No human tongue could tell
The feelings beating in my heart.

What tender thoughts we had,
What hopes, what hearts, Silvia!
How fate and human life
Looked then! Now

Quando sovviemmi di cotanta speme,
Un affetto mi preme
Acerbo e sconsolato,
35  E tornami a doler di mia sventura.
O natura, ò natura,
Perché non rendi poi
Quel che prometti allor? perché di tanto
Inganni i figli tuoi?

40  Tu, pria che l'erbe inaridisse il verno,
Da chiuso morbo combattuta e vinta,
Perivi, o tenerella. E non vedevi
Il fior degli anni tuoi;
Non ti molceva il core
45  La dolce lode or delle negre chiome,
Or degli sguardi innamorati e schivi;
Né teco le compagne ai dì festivi
Ragionavan d'amore.

Anche peria fra poco
50  La speranza mia dolce: agli anni miei
Anche negaro i fati
La giovanezza. Ahi, come,
Come passata sei,
Cara compagna dell'età mia nova,
55  Mia lacrimata speme!
Questo è quel mondo? questi
I diletti, l'amor, l'opre, gli eventi,
Onde cotanto ragionammo insieme?
Questa la sorte dell' umane genti?
60  All'apparir del vero
Tu, misera, cadesti; e con la mano
La fredda morte ed una tomba ignuda
Mostravi di lontano.

1828

When I think of all that hope
I'm bitterly stricken,
Beyond consolation, and begin
Lamenting again my own misfortunes.
Ah, nature, nature, why
Can you never make good
Your promises? Why
Must you so deceive your own children?

Before winter had withered the grass,
You were dying, dear girl,
Struck and cut down by blind disease.
And you didn't see your years
Break into blossom, nor ever felt
Your heart melt
Under honeyed praise of your jet-black tresses
Or the shy enamored light in your eyes.
And never did your friends spend Sundays
Whispering with you, all about love.

And soon, too, my own fond hopes
Withered and died: my youth, too,
The fates cut off. Ah,
Alas how you've faded,
My tearstained hope, belovèd
Comrade of those spring days!
Is this the world we imagined? These
The pleasures, love, adventures
We two together talked and talked of?
Is this what it means to be born human?
At the very first touch of things as they are
You shriveled, poor thing,
And with raised hand pointed away
To the cold figure of death
And an unmarked grave.

# IL PASSERO SOLITARIO

D'in su la vetta della torre antica,
Passero solitario, alla campagna
Cantando vai finché non more il giorno;
Ed erra l'armonia per questa valle.
5 Primavera d'intorno
Brilla nell'aria, e per li campi esulta,
Sì ch'a mirarla intenerisce il core.
Odi greggi belar, muggire armenti;
10 Gli altri augelli contenti, a gara insieme
Per lo libero ciel fan mille giri,
Pur festeggiando il lor tempo migliore:
Tu pensoso in disparte il tutto miri;
15 Non compagni, non voli,
Non ti cal d'allegria, schivi gli spassi;
Canti, e così trapassi
Dell'anno e di tua vita il più bel fiore.

Oimè, quanto somiglia
20 Al tuo costume il mio! Sollazzo e riso,
Della novella età dolce famiglia,
E te german di giovinezza, amore,
Sospiro acerbo de' provetti giorni,
Non curo, io non so come; anzi da loro
25 Quasi fuggo lontano;
Quasi romito, e strano
Al mio loco natio,
Passo del viver mio la primavera.
Questo giorno, ch'omai cede alla sera,
30 Festeggiar si costuma al nostro borgo.
Odi per lo sereno un suon di squilla,
Odi spesso un tonar di ferree canne,
Che rimbomba lontan di villa in villa.

# THE SOLITARY THRUSH

Perched on top of that old tower,
You sing as long as daylight lasts,
The sweet sound of you winding
Round and round the valley.
Spring shimmers
In the air, comes with a green rush
Through the open fields, is a sight
To soften any heart. You can hear
Sheep bleating, bellowing cattle,
While the other birds swoop and wheel
Cheerily round the wide blue sky,
Having the time of their lives together.
Like an outsider, lost in thought,
You are looking on at it all:
Neither companions nor wild flights
Fire your heart; games like these
Mean nothing to you. You sing,
And in singing spend the best
Part of your life and the passing year.

Ah, how these habits of mine
Are just like yours! Whatever the reason,
I haven't time for the light heart and laughter
Belonging to youth, nor any time
For you, youth's own companion, love,
Which later brings many a bitter sigh.
In truth I'm a fugitive from it all
And, still young, I all but live
The life of a hermit, a stranger even
In the place I was born.
This day already dwindling into dusk
Is a feast in these parts. You can hear
The bells ring round a clear sky
And a far-off thunder of guns
Booming and booming from farm to farm.

Tutta vestita a festa
35 La gioventù del loco
Lascia le case, e per le vie si spande;
E mira ed è mirata, e in cor s'allegra.
Io, solitario in questa
Rimota parte alla campagna uscendo,
40 Ogni diletto e gioco
Indugio in altro tempo; e intanto il guardo
Steso nell'aria aprica
Mi fere il sol, che tra lontani monti,
Dopo il giorno sereno,
45 Cadendo si dilegua, e par che dica
Che la beata gioventù vien meno.

Tu, solingo augellin, venuto a sera
Del viver che daranno a te le stelle,
Certo del tuo costume
50 Non ti dorrai; che di natura è frutto
Ogni vostra vaghezza.
A me, se di vecchiezza
La detestata soglia
Evitar non impetro,
55 Quando muti questi occhi all'altrui core,
E lor fia vòto il mondo, e il dì futuro
Del dì presente più noioso e tetro,
Che parrà di tal voglia?
Che di quest'anni miei? che di me stesso?
60 Ahi pentirommi, e spesso,
Ma sconsolato, volgerommi indietro.

1829–30

All dressed up in their Sunday best,
The young who live around here
Leave their houses and stroll the roads,
Looking and looked at, joy in their hearts.
Alone in this remote corner,
I walk out all by myself,
Putting off pleasure, postponing play:
And gazing about at the radiant air
I'm struck by how the sinking sun
After a day as perfect as this one
Melts among the distant hills,
And seems to say
That blessed youth itself is fading.

Solitary little singer, when you
Reach the evening of those days
Which the stars have numbered for you,
You'll not grieve, surely,
For the life you've led, since even
The slightest twist of your will
Is nature's way. But to me,
If I fail to escape
Loathsome old age—
When these eyes will mean nothing
To any other heart, the world be nothing
But a blank to them,
Each day more desolate, every day
Darker than the one before—what then
Will this longing for solitude
Seem like to me? What then
Will these years, or even I myself,
Seem to have been? Alas,
I'll be sick with regret, and over and over,
But inconsolable, looking back.

# LE RICORDANZE

Vaghe stelle dell'Orsa, io non credea
Tornare ancor per uso a contemplarvi
Sul paterno giardino scintillanti,
E ragionar con voi dalle finestre
5    Di questo albergo ove abitai fanciullo,
E delle gioie mie vidi la fine.
Quante immagini un tempo, e quante fole
Creommi nel pensier l'aspetto vostro
E delle luci a voi compagne! allora
10   Che, tacito, seduto in verde zolla,
Delle sere io solea passar gran parte
Mirando il cielo, ed ascoltando il canto
Della rana rimota alla campagna!
E la lucciola errava appo le siepi
15   E in su l'aiuole, susurrando al vento
I viali odorati, ed i cipressi
Là nella selva; e sotto al patrio tetto
Sonavan voci alterne, e le tranquille
Opre de' servi. E che pensieri immensi,
20   Che dolci sogni mi spirò la vista
Di quel lontano mar, quei monti azzurri,
Che di qua scopro, e che varcare un giorno
Io mi pensava, arcani mondi, arcana
Felicità fingendo al viver mio!
25   Ignaro del mio fato, e quante volte
Questa mia vita dolorosa e nuda
Volentier con la morte avrei cangiato.

Né mi diceva il cor che l'età verde
Sarei dannato a consumare in questo
30   Natio borgo selvaggio, intra una gente
Zotica, vil; cui nomi strani, e spesso
Argomento di riso e di trastullo
Son dottrina e saper; che m'odia e fugge,
Per invidia non già, che non mi tiene

# MEMORIES

Glimmering stars of the Great Bear,
I never thought I'd be back to see you
Shining down on my father's garden,
Nor talk to you ever again from the windows
Of this house where I spent my childhood
And saw the last of my happiness vanish.
What fancies you quickened in me once—
You and all your glittering sisters—
When, lying on a bank of grass, I'd gaze
Up at the sky in silence each evening
And listen to the song the frogs were singing
In the distant fields. Fireflies
Flitted among hedges and flowerbeds,
While the cypress woods and fragrant avenues of trees
Were whispering in the wind. I could hear
The murmur of voices float back and forth
In my father's house, and the low sounds
The servants made going about their chores.
What vast imaginings and vivid dreams
Were kindled by the far-off sight of the sea
And those blue mountains I can see from here
And which I thought I'd cross some day—
Conjuring up mysterious worlds
And a future full of secret joys, knowing
Nothing of whatever might lie in store,
Nor yet how often I'd gladly have swapped
This bereft wretched life of mine for death.

Nor did I, then, ever let on to myself
I was doomed to waste my life in this
Barbarous place where I was born,
Surrounded by a crowd of crude know-nothings
Who mock and jeer at what's beyond them—
Wisdom and knowledge—and hate me
And shun my company, not from envy—

35    Maggior di sé, ma perché tale estima
      Ch'io mi tenga in cor mio, sebben di fuori
      A persona giammai non ne fo segno.
      Qui passo gli anni, abbandonato, occulto,
      Senz'amor, senza vita; ed aspro a forza
40    Tra lo stuol de' malevoli divengo:
      Qui di pietà mi spoglio e di virtudi,
      E sprezzator degli uomini mi rendo,
      Per la greggia c'ho appresso: e intanto vola
      Il caro tempo giovanil; più caro
45    Che la fama e l'allor, più che la pura
      Luce del giorno, e lo spirar: ti perdo
      Senza un diletto, inutilmente, in questo
      Soggiorno disumano, intra gli affanni,
      O dell'arida vita unico fiore.

50    Viene il vento recando il suon dell'ora
      Dalla torre del borgo. Era conforto
      Questo suon, mi rimembra, alle mie notti,
      Quando fanciullo, nella buia stanza,
      Per assidui terrori io vigilava,
55    Sospirando il mattin. Qui non è cosa
      Ch'io vegga o senta, onde un'immagin dentro
      Non torni, e un dolce rimembrar non sorga.
      Dolce per sé; ma con dolor sottentra
      Il pensier del presente, un van desio
60    Del passato, ancor tristo, e il dire: io fui.
      Quella loggia colà, volta agli estremi
      Raggi del dì; queste dipinte mura,
      Quei figurati armenti, e il sol che nasce
      Su romita campagna, agli ozi miei
65    Porser mille diletti allor che al fianco
      M'era, parlando, il mio possente errore
      Sempre, ov'io fossi. In queste sale antiche,
      Al chiaror delle nevi, intorno a queste
      Ampie finestre sibilando il vento,

Since, in their eyes, I can be no better
Than they are themselves—but just because
(Though I show no sign at all)
They imagine I think so in my heart. Here
I spend years—loveless, alone, buried alive,
And growing bitter as a matter of course,
Cast among this pack of begrudgers. Here—
Because of whom I have to herd with—
I lose every last shred of civility,
Am stripped of every decent feeling,
And become a despiser of mankind,
Whilst all the while my priceless youth—
More precious than any laurel crown,
Dearer than daylight or breath itself—
Takes flight. Sunk among miseries
In this inhuman place, living to no purpose
And lacking all joy, it's youth I lose,
The one and only flower that blooms
In this desert that we call life.

The wind brings the sound of the town-hall clock
Striking the hour. I remember the comfort
It brought me as a boy, those nights I lay
Awake and frightened in the dark, sighing
For daylight. Whatever I hear or see in this place
Harbors an image or a happy memory.
Happy in itself, but then, with a shock of pain,
The present floods back, and a fruitless
Longing for the past, sad as it's been, and the words,
*I was.* That loggia facing the last flush of sunset,
These ceilings with their painted scenes
Of pastoral flocks, herds of cattle, dawn
Brightening a deserted landscape—all
Delighted my daydreams then, when still,
Wherever I went, my strong-winged fancy
Was always beside me, filling
This head of mine with talk. By snowlight
In these old rooms, with the wind
Whistling against great bay windows,

70 Rimbombaro i sollazzi e le festose
Mie voci al tempo che l'acerbo, indegno
Mistero delle cose a noi si mostra
Pien di dolcezza; indelibata, intera
Il garzoncel, come inesperto amante,
75 La sua vita ingannevole vagheggia,
E celeste beltà fingendo ammira.

O speranze, speranze; ameni inganni
Della mia prima età! sempre, parlando,
Ritorno a voi; che per andar di tempo,
80 Per variar d'affetti e di pensieri,
Obbliarvi non so. Fantasmi, intendo,
Son la gloria e l'onor; diletti e beni
Mero desio; non ha la vita un frutto,
Inutile miseria. E sebben vòti
85 Son gli anni miei, sebben deserto, oscuro
Il mio stato mortal, poco mi toglie
La fortuna, ben veggo. Ahi, ma qualvolta
A voi ripenso, o mie speranze antiche,
Ed a quel caro immaginar mio primo;
90 Indi riguardo il viver mio sì vile
E sì dolente, e che la morte è quello
Che di cotanta speme oggi m'avanza;
Sento serrarmi il cor, sento ch'al tutto
Consolarmi non so del mio destino.
95 E quando pur questa invocata morte
Sarammi allato, e sarà giunto il fine
Della sventura mia; quando la terra
Mi fia straniera valle, e dal mio sguardo
Fuggirà l'avvenir; di voi per certo
100 Risovverrammi; e quell'imago ancora
Sospirar mi farà, farammi acerbo
L'esser vissuto indarno, e la dolcezza
Del dì fatal tempererà d'affanno.

E già nel primo giovanil tumulto
105 Di contenti, d'angosce e di desio,
Morte chiamai più volte, e lungamente

My games and wild cries set echoes ringing,
Ringing through that time in our lives
When the mean and bitter mystery of things
Seems to brim with sweetness: when, spellbound,
A boy will gaze like a raw young lover
At his untried, untouched, untrustworthy life,
And hold his breath at that heavenly beauty
He, in his own imagination, is creating.

Ah, the hopes I had as a child, you hopes
And childish enchantments! My talk always
Circles back to you: in spite of time, in spite
Of how the mind changes, changes of heart,
I cannot forget you. Honor and glory
Are will-o'-the-wisps; the pleasures of life
Lie only in desire; existence is pointless,
Suffering useless; and even though
My life is wretched, my days and nights
Nothing but a blank, I know that fortune
Doesn't, in fact, deprive me of much. But
Whenever I think of you, old hopes and
Golden dreams of youth, and then behold
My life as it is—thus troubled, cast down,
Not one of those high hopes left but death—
I feel my heart slam shut, and can find
No consolation for the life I've been given.
And when that wished-for death at last
Comes to put an end to all my anguish,
When the world will seem an alien place
And the future fly from my sight, I know
I'll bring you all to mind once more
And the thought of you will still make me sigh,
Will make me bitter that I'll have lived
My life in vain, tempering with real grief
The expected sweet release of death.

And even in youth's first whirlwind
Of pain and pleasure and desire, I'd often
Call on death, and sit for hours at a time

Mi sedetti colà su la fontana
Pensoso di cessar dentro quell'acque
La speme e il dolor mio. Poscia, per cieco
110 Malor, condotto della vita in forse,
Piansi la bella giovanezza, e il fiore
De' miei poveri dì, che sì per tempo
Cadeva: e spesso all'ore tarde, assiso
Sul conscio letto, dolorosamente
115 Alla fioca lucerna poetando,
Lamentai co' silenzi e con la notte
Il fuggitivo spirto, ed a me stesso
In sul languir cantai funereo canto.

Chi rimembrar vi può senza sospiri,
120 O primo entrar di giovinezza, o giorni
Vezzosi, inenarrabili, allor quando
Al rapito mortal primieramente
Sorridon le donzelle; a gara intorno
Ogni cosa sorride; invidia tace,
125 Non desta ancora ovver benigna; e quasi
(Inusitata maraviglia!) il mondo
La destra soccorrevole gli porge,
Scusa gli errori suoi, festeggia il novo
Suo venir nella vita, ed inchinando
130 Mostra che per signor l'accolga e chiami?
Fugaci giorni! a somigliar d'un lampo
Son dileguati. E qual mortale ignaro
Di sventura esser può, se a lui già scorsa
Quella vaga stagion, se il suo buon tempo,
135 Se giovanezza, ahi giovanezza, è spenta?

O Nerina! e di te forse non odo
Questi luoghi parlar? caduta forse
Dal mio pensier sei tu? Dove sei gita,
140 Che qui sola di te la ricordanza
Trovo, dolcezza mia? Più non ti vede
Questa terra natal: quella finestra,
Ond'eri usata favellarmi, ed onde
Mesto riluce delle stelle il raggio,

By that pond over there, thinking to give
All my hopes and my sufferings at once
A watery grave. But later, when blind disease
Brought me to the brink of death itself,
I shed salt tears for blossoming youth
And the flower, fast fading, of my stricken days.
And often, sitting up late, tossing on my bed,
Scribbling sad odes by shadowy lamplight,
I'd pour out lamentations to night and silence
For the quick spirit slipping away, and sing
To my languishing self a song of death.

Who can remember you without sighing,
You first stirrings of youth, days bewitching
Beyond description, when girls start smiling
At the lovestruck boy, and everything
Seems eager to be kind; and even envy—
Either still asleep or in a friendly mood—
Keeps quiet, and the world (imagine!)
Almost extends a helping hand, forgives
His mistakes, rejoices at his fresh
Setting-out in life, and bends to him
As its lord and master? Days
Quick as lightning, vanished in a flash!
And who can be a stranger to misfortune
Once that dreamtime is gone for good, once
His sunny days and youth—ah, youth itself!—
Are spent, quenched, quite grown cold?

And you, Nerina! Do I not hear
These places say your name? could you
Have vanished from my thoughts? Where
Have you gone, my dear, that here I find
Only your memory? Your own birthplace
Sees you no more: that very window
You'd talk to me from is empty, reflecting
Only rueful starlight. Where are you, that I

145 È deserta. Ove sei, che più non odo
La tua voce sonar, siccome un giorno,
Quando soleva ogni lontano accento
Del labbro tuo, ch'a me giungesse, il volto
Scolorarmi? Altro tempo. I giorni tuoi
150 Furo, mio dolce amor. Passasti. Ad altri
Il passar per la terra oggi è sortito,
E l'abitar questi odorati colli.
Ma rapida passasti, e come un sogno
Fu la tua vita. Ivi danzando, in fronte
155 La gioia ti splendea, splendea negli occhi
Quel confidente immaginar, quel lume
Di gioventù, quando spegneali il fato,
E giacevi. Ahi Nerina! In cor mi regna
L'antico amor. Se a feste anco talvolta,
160 Se a radunanze io movo, infra me stesso
Dico: o Nerina, a radunanze, a feste
Tu non ti acconci più, tu più non movi.
Se torna maggio, e ramoscelli e suoni
Van gli amanti recando alle fanciulle,
165 Dico: Nerina mia, per te non torna
Primavera giammai, non torna amore.
Ogni giorno sereno, ogni fiorita
Piaggia ch'io miro, ogni goder ch'io sento,
Dico: Nerina or più non gode; i campi,
170 L'aria non mira. Ahi! tu passasti, eterno
Sospiro mio: passasti: e fia compagna
D'ogni mio vago immaginar, di tutti
I miei teneri sensi, i tristi e cari
Moti del cor, la rimembranza acerba.

1829

No longer can hear your voice as I used to,
When the faintest sound that came from your lips
Made my face grow pale? Other days. Yours,
Dear heart, are done. You departed. Now
It is others' turn to walk in the world
And dwell among these fragrant hills.
But you, you hurried away, your life
Like a dream. There, you were dancing there,
Your face on fire with joy, your eyes
Shining with that steady light of youth
That said the world was at your feet,
When fate put out the blaze
And you lay down. Ah, Nerina! In my heart
I feel the old love beating. And now,
If ever I go to a party or where there's dancing,
I think to myself —*You, Nerina,*
*Don't dress up for parties anymore,*
*You go to no more dances.*
And when May comes round again, and the boys
Bring their sweethearts songs and flowering branches,
I say to myself —*Ah, Nerina, spring*
*Doesn't come again for you, nor ever again*
*Comes love.* Each summer's day I see,
And every flowering bank I see, whenever
Any pleasure stirs, I say —*Nerina*
*Feels pleasure in nothing now: she sees*
*Neither the fields nor the shining air.*
Ah, my dear, for whom I shall never
Stop sighing, away you went, you went away,
And all my fancies and tender feelings, all
These sweet unhappy stirrings of my heart,
Keep company with nothing but the bitter memory.

# LA QUIETE
# DOPO LA TEMPESTA

Passata è la tempesta:
Odo augelli far festa, e la gallina,
Tornata in su la via,
Che ripete il suo verso. Ecco il sereno
5  Rompe là da ponente, alla montagna;
Sgombrasi la campagna,
E chiaro nella valle il fiume appare.
Ogni cor si rallegra, in ogni lato
Risorge il romorio,
10  Torna il lavoro usato.
L'artigiano a mirar l'umido cielo,
Con l'opra in man, cantando,
Fassi in su l'uscio; a prova
Vien fuor la femminetta a còr dell'acqua
15  Della novella piova;
E l'erbaiuol rinnova
Di sentiero in sentiero
Il grido giornaliero.
Ecco il sol che ritorna, ecco sorride
20  Per li poggi e le ville. Apre i balconi,
Apre terrazzi e logge la famiglia:
E, dalla via corrente, odi lontano
Tintinnio di sonagli; il carro stride
Del passeggier che il suo cammin ripiglia.

25  Si rallegra ogni core.
Sì dolce, sì gradita
Quand'è, com'or, la vita?
Quando con tanto amore
L'uomo a' suoi studi intende?
30  O torna all'opre? o cosa nova imprende?

# THE CALM &

## AFTER THE STORM

The storm has blown over:
I can hear the happy chatter of birds,
And the hen out on the road again
Cacackling her one phrase. Look
How blue breaks over the mountains
From the west, the fields grow clear,
And the river gleams in the valley.
People feel lighthearted, sounds of life
Spill out of every corner,
Things are getting back to normal.
With a piece of work in hand
The craftsman stands
And sings in his own doorway,
So he can see the glistening sky;
Housewives hurry to gather
The first pails of fresh rainwater;
And from street to narrow street
The vegetable-seller again
Raises his daily cry. And here
Comes the sun once more, smiling
On all the houses and the little hills.
Families throw windows wide open,
Open wide their terraces and porches,
And from the high road you can catch
A distant jingle of harness
As the stagecoach sets off again, heaving and creaking.

Every heart is light with joy.
Can our life ever be sweeter
Or more complete
Than at this moment? Will a man
Ever bend with such relish
To his books, get on with his work,

Quando de' mali suoi men si ricorda?
Piacer figlio d'affanno;
Gioia vana, ch'è frutto
Del passato timore, onde si scosse
35    E paventò la morte
Chi la vita abborria;
Onde in lungo tormento,
Fredde, tacite, smorte,
Sudàr le genti e palpitàr, vedendo
40    Mossi alle nostre offese
Folgori, nembi e vento.

O natura cortese,
Son questi i doni tuoi,
Questi i diletti sono
45    Che tu porgi ai mortali. Uscir di pena
È diletto fra noi.
Pene tu spargi a larga mano; il duolo
Spontaneo sorge: e di piacer, quel tanto
Che per mostro e miracolo talvolta
50    Nasce d'affanno, è gran guadagno. Umana
Prole cara agli eterni! assai felice
Se respirar ti lice
D'alcun dolor; beata
Se te d'ogni dolor morte risana.

1829

Start something new? Or ever
Think less of his own distress?
Pleasure born of pain;
Insubstantial joy that flows
From the fright that's come and gone,
Which made even him who loathed life
Shiver all over and fear death—
It's this that causes people to shake
In mortal agony, break into cold sweat,
Petrified, speechless, pale as ghosts,
Thinking thunder and lightning and wind and rain
Stirred up on purpose to hurt us.

Gracious nature, these
Are the gifts you grant us,
These the favors you lavish
On mortal men and women. For us,
Pleasure means escape from pain.
Sufferings you scatter
With prodigal hand; unhappiness
Needs no prompting; and that
One touch or two of joy
That like a miracle or nine-day marvel
Springs from sorrow
Is our rich reward. Mankind,
Darling of the gods! Happy to find
Some breathing space
Between griefs; and truly blest
If all your ills are cured by death.

# IL SABATO DEL VILLAGGIO 🌿

La donzelletta vien dalla campagna,
In sul calar del sole,
Col suo fascio dell'erba, e reca in mano
Un mazzolin di rose e di viole,
5    Onde, siccome suole,
Ornare ella si appresta
Dimani, al dì di festa, il petto e il crine.
Siede con le vicine
Su la scala a filar la vecchierella,
10   Incontro là dove si perde il giorno;
E novellando vien del suo buon tempo,
Quando ai dì della festa ella si ornava,
Ed ancor sana e snella
Solea danzar la sera intra di quei
15   Ch'ebbe compagni dell'età più bella.
Già tutta l'aria imbruna,
Torna azzurro il sereno, e tornan l'ombre
Giù da' colli e da' tetti,
Al biancheggiar della recente luna.
20   Or la squilla dà segno
Della festa che viene;
Ed a quel suon diresti
Che il cor si riconforta.
I fanciulli gridando
25   Su la piazzuola in frotta,
E qua e là saltando,
Fanno un lieto romore:
E intanto riede alla sua parca mensa,
Fischiando, il zappatore,
30   E seco pensa al dí del suo riposo.

Poi quando intorno è spenta ogni altra face,
E tutto l'altro tace,
Odi il martel picchiare, odi la sega

# SATURDAY IN THE VILLAGE ❧

Just at that hour when the sun is setting,
The young girl comes in from the fields
With an armful of fresh grass
And a little bunch of violets and wild roses
To bind in her hair
And pin at her breast
Tomorrow, as she does every Sunday.
On her own front steps the old woman
Sits spinning with her neighbors,
Facing the sun as it sinks in the west.
She prattles on about the good old days
When she too would dress up for Sunday,
And how—still quick and trim—
She'd dance the evening away
With all those boyfriends she had
In her shining youth. Already
Dusk is thickening the air,
The sky turns deep blue, shadows
Stretch from the hills and tilting roofs
In the blanched light of the rising moon.
And now the pealing bell tells us
Tomorrow is Sunday,
And at that sound you'd say
The heart took comfort.
Dashing all over the little piazza
And shouting their heads off,
A flock of boys makes a happy racket,
While the farmhand goes home whistling
To his bit of supper,
Thinking about his day of rest.

Then, when every other light is out
And there isn't another sound,
You'll hear the carpenter's saw,
You'll hear his hammer

Del legnaiuol, che veglia
35   Nella chiusa bottega alla lucerna,
E s'affretta, e s'adopra
Di fornir l'opra anzi il chiarir dell'alba.

Questo di sette è il più gradito giorno,
Pien di speme e di gioia:
40   Diman tristezza e noia
Recheran l'ore, ed al travaglio usato
Ciascuno in suo pensier farà ritorno.

Garzoncello scherzoso,
Cotesta età fiorita
45   E come un giorno d'allegrezza pieno,
Giorno chiaro, sereno,
Che precorre alla festa di tua vita.
Godi, fanciullo mio; stato soave,
Stagion lieta è cotesta.
50   Altro dirti non vo'; ma la tua festa
Ch'anco tardi a venir non ti sia grave.

1829

Banging from the shuttered shop,
Where, by lamplight, he sweats and strains
To finish a job before break of day.

Of all the seven days in the week
This one gets the warmest welcome,
Full of hope, as it is, and joy.
Tomorrow the hours will be leaden
With emptiness and melancholy,
Everybody going back in his mind
To the daily grind.

Young lad, larking about,
This blossom-time of yours
Is like a day of pure delight,
A cloudless blue day
Before the feast of your life.
Enjoy it, little one, for this
Is a state of bliss, a glad season.
I'll say no more, only
Don't fret if your Sunday
Seems a long time coming.

# CANTO NOTTURNO DI UN 🐎

# PASTORE ERRANTE DELL' ASIA

Che fai tu, luna, in ciel? dimmi, che fai,
Silenziosa luna?
Sorgi la sera, e vai,
Contemplando i deserti; indi ti posi.
5    Ancor non sei tu paga
Di riandare i sempiterni calli?
Ancor non prendi a schivo, ancor sei vaga
Di mirar queste valli?
Somiglia alla tua vita
10   La vita del pastore.
Sorge in sul primo albore
Move la greggia oltre pel campo, e vede
Greggi, fontane ed erbe;
Poi stanco si riposa in su la sera:
15   Altro mai non ispera.
Dimmi, o luna: a che vale
Al pastor la sua vita,
La vostra vita a voi? dimmi: ove tende
Questo vagar mio breve,
20   Il tuo corso immortale?

Vecchierel bianco, infermo,
Mezzo vestito e scalzo,
Con gravissimo fascio in su le spalle,
Per montagna e per valle,
25   Per sassi acuti, ed alta rena, e fratte,
Al vento, alla tempesta, e quando avvampa
L'ora, e quando poi gela,
Corre via, corre, anela,
Varca torrenti e stagni,
30   Cade, risorge, e più e più s'affretta,
Senza posa o ristoro,
Lacero, sanguinoso; infin ch'arriva

# NIGHT SONG OF A

## NOMADIC SHEPHERD IN ASIA

Moon, moon of silence, what are you doing,
Tell me what you're doing in the sky?
You rise in the evening-time and go
Brooding over barren open country,
Then sink to rest. Haven't you had enough
Of traveling those everlasting paths?
Aren't you tired of gazing
Down on these valleys, or can you still
See something in them? A shepherd's life
Is like the life you live:
Rising at first light
He leads his flock over the fields, and sees
Flocks, streams, tracts of grass;
At evening he goes, tired, to his rest:
He never hopes for anything else.
Tell me, what use
Is the shepherd's life to the shepherd
Or yours to you? To what end, tell me,
Are these brief wanderings of mine,
Or your voyage that never ends?

A ragged old man,
Ailing, white-haired, barefoot,
Bent under a heavy load,
Hurries across mountains, through valleys,
Over sharp rocks, deep sands, and briary wastes,
Hurries in wind and rain,
Under blazing sun, in bitter chill,
Hurrying faster, gasping for breath,
Crossing swamps and flooded streams,
Tumbling, stumbling, on he hurries,
No food, no water, not a minute's rest,
All bloodied and torn to bits

Colà dove la via
E dove il tanto affaticar fu volto:
35   Abisso orrido, immenso,
Ov'ei precipitando, il tutto obblia.
Vergine luna, tale
È la vita mortale.

Nasce l'uomo a fatica,
40   Ed è rischio di morte il nascimento.
Prova pena e tormento
Per prima cosa; e in sul principio stesso
La madre e il genitore
Il prende a consolar dell'esser nato.
45   Poi che crescendo viene,
L'uno e l'altro il sostiene, e via pur sempre
Con atti e con parole
Studiasi fargli core,
E consolarlo dell'umano stato:
50   Altro ufficio più grato
Non si fa da parenti alla lor prole.
Ma perché dare al sole,
Perché reggere in vita
Chi poi di quella consolar convenga?
55   Se la vita è sventura,
Perché da noi si dura?
Intatta luna, tale
È lo stato mortale.
Ma tu mortal non sei,
60   E forse del mio dir poco ti cale.

Pur tu, solinga, eterna peregrina,
Che sì pensosa sei, tu forse intendi
Questo viver terreno,
Il patir nostro, il sospirar, che sia;
65   Che sia questo morir, questo supremo
Scolorar del sembiante,
E perir dalla terra, e venir meno
Ad ogni usata, amante compagnia.

Till he reaches his journey's end at last
And the end of all those fierce exertions:
A fearsome, bottomless abyss
Into which he flings himself,
Obliterating everything.
Bright, unspotted moon,
That's human life for you.

A man comes struggling into the world;
His birth is in the shadow of death;
Pain and suffering
Are his first discoveries;
And from that point
His mother and his father try
To console him for having been born.
As he grows older—supporting him
By word and deed—the two of them
Do their best to keep his heart up,
Consoling him for his human condition:
Surely there's no kinder office
Parents could perform for offspring.
But why bring into the light of day,
Why protect the life of a creature
Who needs to be consoled for life?
If life is nothing but misfortune,
What's the point of bearing it at all?
And this, unblemished moon,
Is the mortal state of man.
But you're no mortal, and you may
Give little heed to what I say.

Yet a solitary, ceaseless wanderer like you,
Brooder as you are, might understand
The lives we lead on earth,
The ways we suffer, why we sigh, what dying means:
That last warm trace of color fading
As we perish from the face of the earth
And leave behind us
All our old friends and loving company.

E tu certo comprendi
70   Il perché delle cose, e vedi il frutto
Del mattin, della sera,
Del tacito, infinito andar del tempo.
Tu sai, tu certo, a qual suo dolce amore
Rida la primavera,
75   A chi giovi l'ardore, e che procacci
Il verno co' suoi ghiacci.
Mille cose sai tu, mille discopri,
Che son celate al semplice pastore.
Spesso quand'io ti miro
80   Star così muta in sul deserto piano,
Che, in suo giro lontano, al ciel confina;
Ovver con la mia greggia
Seguirmi viaggiando a mano a mano;
E quando miro in cielo arder le stelle;
85   Dico fra me pensando:
A che tante facelle?
Che fa l'aria infinita, e quel profondo
Infinito seren? che vuol dir questa
Solitudine immensa? ed io che sono?
90   Così meco ragiono: e della stanza
Smisurata e superba,
E dell'innumerabile famiglia;
Poi di tanto adoprar, di tanti moti
D'ogni celeste, ogni terrena cosa,
95   Girando senza posa,
Per tornar sempre là donde son mosse;
Uso alcuno, alcun frutto
Indovinar non so. Ma tu per certo,
Giovinetta immortal, conosci il tutto.
100   Questo io conosco e sento,
Che degli eterni giri,
Che dell'esser mio frale,
Qualche bene o contento
Avrà fors'altri: a me la vita è male.

105   O greggia mia che posi, oh te beata,
Che la miseria tua, credo, non sai!

And indeed you know right well
Why things happen, what morning means
And evening, and the ever-winding silent
Stream of time. You, you surely, know
On what sweet beloved of its own
The springtime smiles, whom the burning
Sun of summer cheers, who finds delight
In winter with its snow and ice.
You know a thousand things like these
And understand a thousand more
Hidden from a simple shepherd.
Many a time when I see you hanging
So silent above the flat unbroken plain
That stretches to touch the very edge of the sky,
Or following me as I go with my sheep
And keeping pace with me as I
Behold in heaven the fiery stars, I ask myself:
*Why so many blazing torches?*
*What's the point of the endless air*
*Or the infinite deep reaches of sky?*
*What does this huge solitude mean? Or what am I?*
I pester myself with questions like these
About the vast and splendid
Dwelling-place of space and the teeming
Family of stars, and I just can't see
The point or purpose
Of all the mighty works and motions
Of everything in the heavens and earth
Ceaselessly wheeling and wheeling back
To where they started. But you for sure,
Immortal girl, you know it all.
All I know, feelingly, is this:
That these vast, never-ending cycles
Or this little existence of mine
*May* bring about some good, for others;
For me, life is nothing but trouble and pain.

You lucky sheep, taking your ease,
Lucky to know nothing, I believe,
Of the wretchedness in your own lives.

Quanta invidia ti porto!
Non sol perché d'affanno
Quasi libera vai;
110   Ch'ogni stento, ogni danno,
Ogni estremo timor subito scordi;
Ma più perché giammai tedio non provi.
Quando tu siedi all'ombra, sovra l'erbe,
Tu se' queta e contenta;
115   E gran parte dell'anno
Senza noia consumi in quello stato.
Ed io pur seggo sovra l'erbe, all'ombra,
E un fastidio m'ingombra
La mente, ed uno spron quasi mi punge
120   Sì che, sedendo, più che mai son lunge
Da trovar pace o loco.
E pur nulla non bramo,
E non ho fino a qui cagion di pianto.
Quel che tu goda o quanto,
125   Non so già dir; ma fortunata sei.
Ed io godo ancor poco,
O greggia mia, né di ciò sol mi lagno.
Se tu parlar sapessi, io chiederei:
Dimmi: perché giacendo
130   A bell'agio, ozioso,
S'appaga ogni animale;
Me, s'io giaccio in riposo, il tedio assale?

Forse s'avess'io l'ale
Da volar su le nubi,
135   E noverar le stelle ad una ad una,
O come il tuono errar di giogo in giogo,
Più felice sarei, dolce mia greggia,
Più felice sarei, candida luna.
O forse erra dal vero,
140   Mirando all'altrui sorte, il mio pensiero:
Forse in qual forma, in quale
Stato che sia, dentro covile o cuna,
È funesto a chi nasce il dì natale.

1829–30

How I envy you this! Not just because you are
All but free from fretful care, quickly forgetting
Your terror, your hunger, every ache,
But more because you never feel
Any weariness of spirit. When you
Lie down in the grassy shade
You're quiet, quite at peace,
And you pass a great part of the year
Unperturbed, in just that state.
But when I lie down in the grassy shade
A heaviness presses against my mind
As if I'm being somehow needled by something,
So lying there I am farther than ever
From finding any peace or place of rest. And yet
I want for nothing at all,
And nothing till now gives me cause for tears.
I neither know what nor yet how deep
Might be your joys; but you lead, I know,
Lucky lives. My own life
Has little joy, though that is not
All that grieves me. If you could speak,
I'd ask you this: *Tell me:*
*How can every beast of the field*
*Find pleasure in taking its lazy ease,*
*But if ever I lie down to rest,*
*Melancholy invades my breast?*

Perhaps if I had wings to soar
Over the clouds and count the stars,
Or run like thunder from peak to peak,
I'd be happier, my gentle flock,
I would be happier, radiant moon.
Or maybe I simply miss the truth
In thinking of other lives like this:
Perhaps whatever form it takes
Or wherever it comes to pass—
Lair of beast or baby's cradle—
To that creature being born
Its birth day is a day to mourn.

# THREE

# A SE STESSO 🌿

Or poserai per sempre,
Stanco mio cor. Perì l'inganno estremo,
Ch'eterno io mi credei. Perì. Ben sento,
In noi di cari inganni,
5     Non che la speme, il desiderio è spento.
Posa per sempre. Assai
Palpitasti. Non val cosa nessuna
I moti tuoi, né di sospiri è degna
La terra. Amaro e noia
10    La vita, altro mai nulla; e fango è il mondo.
T'acqueta omai. Dispera
L'ultima volta. Al gener nostro il fato
Non donò che il morire. Omai disprezza
Te, la natura, il brutto
15    Poter che, ascoso, a comun danno impera,
E l'infinita vanità del tutto.

1835

# TO HIMSELF 🌿

Now you will rest, tired heart, forever. Finished
Is your last fantasy, which I felt sure
Would endure forever. It's finished. I know in my bones
That hope and even desire are cold
For any further fond illusions.
Stay easy forever. You've been
Throbbing long enough. Nothing is worth
This beating and beating; the earth
Doesn't deserve a sigh. Life is nothing
But blankness of spirit, a bitter taste, and the world
Mud. Now rest in peace. Despair
For the last time. Fate gave our kind
No gift but death. Cast a cold eye now
On yourself, on nature, on that hideous hidden force
That drives all things to their destruction,
And the infinite *all is vanity* of it all.

# IL TRAMONTO DELLA LUNA

Quale in notte solinga,
Sovra campagne inargentate ed acque,
Là 've zefiro aleggia,
E mille vaghi aspetti
5  E ingannevoli obbietti
Fingon l'ombre lontane
Infra l'onde tranquille
E rami e siepi e collinette e ville;
Giunta al confin del cielo,
10 Dietro Apennino od Alpe, o del Tirreno
Nell'infinito seno
Scende la luna; e si scolora il mondo;
Spariscon l'ombre, ed una
Oscurità la valle e il monte imbruna;
15 Orba la notte resta,
E cantando, con mesta melodia,
L'estremo albor della fuggente luce,
Che dianzi gli fu duce,
Saluta il carrettier dalla sua via;

20 Tal si dilegua, e tale
Lascia l'età mortale
La giovinezza. In fuga
Van l'ombre e le sembianze
Dei dilettosi inganni; e vengon meno
25 Le lontane speranze,
Ove s'appoggia la mortal natura.
Abbandonata, oscura
Resta la vita. In lei porgendo il guardo,
Cerca il confuso viatore invano
30 Del cammin lungo che avanzar si sente
Meta o ragione; e vede
Ch'a sé l'umana sede,
Esso a lei veramente è fatto estrano.

# THE SETTING MOON

As on a lonesome night
Over silvered fields and streams
Where a light breeze rustles
And distant shadows conjure
A thousand will-o'-the-wisps
And phantom shapes
Among the unruffled waves, among
Trees and hedges, hills and houses,
The sailing moon—reaching
The very rim of the sky—sinks
Behind the Alps or Appenines,
Or into the endless heaving
Of the Tyrrhenian Sea, and the world
Grows dim, shadows disappear,
A seamless dark descends
On mountains and valleys, the night
Goes blind, and the wagon-driver
Sings a mournful goodbye
To the last of the fleeting light
That led him safely on; so

Youth fades, and even so
It takes its leave
Of the life of man. The phantoms
And shadows of cherished fancies
Take flight, and future hopes—
Which shore our mortal nature up—
Grow dim. Life remains
Forlorn, bereft of light. Squinting
Into the thickened air, in vain
The baffled traveler strains
To see any purpose or any end
To the long road lying before him,
And sees that he himself and this
Human dwelling-place, the earth,
Are truly strange to one another.

Troppo felice e lieta
35 Nostra misera sorte
Parve lassù, se il giovanile stato,
Dove ogni ben di mille pene è frutto
Durasse tutto della vita il corso.
Troppo mite decreto
40 Quel che sentenzia ogni animale a morte,
S'anco mezza la via
Lor non si desse in pria
Della terribil morte assai più dura.
D'intelletti immortali
45 Degno trovato, estremo
Di tutti i mali, ritrovàr gli eterni
La vecchiezza, ove fosse
Incolume il desio, la speme estinta,
Secche le fonti del piacer, le pene
50 Maggiori sempre, e non più dato il bene.

Voi, collinette e piagge,
Caduto lo splendor che all'occidente
Inargentava della notte il velo,
Orfane ancor gran tempo
55 Non resterete; che dall'altra parte
Tosto vedrete il cielo
Imbiancar novamente, e sorger l'alba:
Alla qual poscia seguitando il sole,
E folgorando intorno
60 Con sue fiamme possenti,
Di lucidi torrenti
Inonderà con voi gli eterei campi.
Ma la vita immortal, poi che la bella
Giovinezza sparì, non si colora
65 D'altra luce giammai, né d'altra aurora.
Vedova è insino al fine; ed alla notte
Che l'altre etadi oscura,
Segno poser gli Dei la sepoltura.

1836

To the gods our wretched human lot
Would seem too trouble-free, too happy,
If youth with its single grain of joy
For every hundredweight of sorrow
Could last a lifetime.
Too lenient that decree
That sentences every animal to die,
Were half the journey of their life
Not worse than dreaded death itself. The gods,
Whose minds remain forever young,
Aptly invented old age
As the worst of evils, old age,
In which desire should be undiminished,
Hope quenched, the springs of pleasure
All dried up, aches and pains
Increasing ever,
Nothing left in life to savor.

You little hills and sandy shores,
Though the brightness in the western sky
That silvered over the stole of night
Is gone, you'll not be left
Orphans long: soon you'll see
The eastern sky grow bright again
And dawn coming; soon the sun
Will fling his fierce refulgent beams
Abroad, flooding you and all the fields of air
With light, torrents of light. But once
Youth with its beauty is gone
No sunshine brightens the life of man,
There is no other dawn. His life remains
Bereft forever; and to lead us into
The night that casts its shadow
Over life's other seasons,
The gods have made
As signpost, terminus, the grave.

# LA GINESTRA 🌿

# O IL FIORE DEL DESERTO

*E gli uomini vollero piuttosto le tenebre che la luce.*
—GIOVANNI 3:19.

Qui su l'arida schiena
Del formidabil monte
Sterminator Vesevo,
La qual null'altro allegra arbor né fiore,
5    Tuoi cespi solitari intorno spargi,
Odorata ginestra,
Contenta dei deserti. Anco ti vidi
De' tuoi steli abbellir l'erme contrade
Che cingon la cittade
10   La qual fu donna de' mortali un tempo,
E del perduto impero
Par che col grave e taciturno aspetto
Faccian fede e ricordo al passeggero.
Or ti riveggo in questo suol, di tristi
15   Lochi e dal mondo abbandonati amante
E d'afflitte fortune ognor compagna.
Questi campi cosparsi
Di ceneri infeconde, e ricoperti
Dell' impietrata lava,
20   Che sotto i passi al peregrin risona;
Dove s'annida e si contorce al sole
La serpe, e dove al noto
Cavernoso covil torna il coniglio;
Fur liete ville e colti,
25   E biondeggiar di spiche, e risonaro
Di muggito d'armenti;
Fur giardini e palagi,
Agli ozi de' potenti
Gradito ospizio; e fur città famose,

# BROOM ✣

# OR THE FLOWER OF THE DESERT

*And men loved darkness rather than light.*

—JOHN 3:19

Here on the naked back
Of this amazing
Exterminator, Mount Vesuvius,
Cheered by no other tree or flower,
You fragrant bushes of broom
Take root in ones and twos,
Making yourselves at home
In these waste places. I've seen
In the deserted countryside near Rome—
Once mistress of the whole world—
The same flowering hedges
Embellish the earth, bearing
Solemn, silent witness for the traveler
To a vanished empire. And now
I see you again, here, faithful
Companions to affliction, lovers
Of sad abandoned corners.
These mountain fields
Covered in cinders, smothered
In solid, footstep-echoing lava,
Where the coiled snake rests
And stretches in the sun, and the rabbit
Keeps close to its rocky warren,
Were once pleasant towns, farmlands
Yellowing with corn, herds
Of bellowing cattle; were once
Orchards and gardens and great houses,
The rich man's retreat and recreation;
And were renowned cities once,

30    Che coi torrenti suoi l'altero monte
Dall'ignea bocca fulminando oppresse
Con gli abitanti insieme. Or tutto intorno
Una ruina involve,
Dove tu siedi, o fior gentile, e quasi
35    I danni altrui commiserando, al cielo
Di dolcissimo odor mandi un profumo,
Che il deserto consola. A queste piagge
Venga colui che d'esaltar con lode
Il nostro stato ha in uso, e vegga quanto
40    È il gener nostro in cura
All'amante natura. E la possanza
Qui con giusta misura
Anco estimar potrà dell'uman seme,
Cui la dura nutrice, ov'ei men teme,
45    Con lieve moto in un momento annulla
In parte, e può con moti
Poco men lievi ancor subitamente
Annichilare in tutto.
Dipinte in queste rive
50    Son dell'umana gente
*Le magnifiche sorti e progressive.*

Qui mira e qui ti specchia,
Secol superbo e sciocco,
Che il calle insino allora
55    Dal risorto pensier segnato innanti
Abbandonasti, e vòlti addietro i passi,
Del ritornar ti vanti,
E procedere il chiami.
Al tuo pargoleggiar gl'ingegni tutti,
Di cui lor sorte rea padre ti fece,
60    Vanno adulando, ancora
Ch'a ludibrio talora
T'abbian fra sé. Non io
Con tal vergogna scenderò sotterra;
Ma il disprezzo piuttosto che si serra
65    Di te nel petto mio,
Mostrato avrò quanto si possa aperto:

Which the towering mountain—
Torrents belching from its fiery mouth—
Overwhelmed with all their inhabitants. Now
Nothing but ruins left
Where this sweet flower takes root
And, it seems, takes pity
On the sufferings of others, filling
The air with fragrance, a touch
Of consolation in the wasteland. Let whoever
Likes to sing the praises of our state
Come to these slopes and see
How loving nature looks after
Our human kind. Here
He may measure exactly
Man's might, which that
Heartless nurse when least expected
Can with a little shrug, in an instant,
Almost obliterate, and with
Some barely bigger shudderings
Just as abruptly bring to nothing.
Inscribed on these slopes you'll find
Mankind's
*Splendid and progressive destiny.*

Look and see yourself here,
You proud, vain, ignorant century,
You who abandoned the trail
Blazed by an enlightened age
And traveled backwards,
All puffed up, calling it progress.
Our learnèd men—whose bad luck
Was to be born in times like these—
Flatter your foolishness in public,
Even if sometimes, among themselves,
They make a laughingstock of you. But I
Won't take such shame to the grave:
Instead I'll let the whole world know
The scorn for you that scalds my heart,
Although I'm sure oblivion buries

Bench'io sappia che obblio
Preme chi troppo all'età propria increbbe.
Di questo mal, che teco
70 Mi fia comune, assai finor mi rido.
Libertà vai sognando, e servo a un tempo
Vuoi di novo il pensiero,
Sol per cui risorgemmo
Dalla barbarie in parte, e per cui solo
75 Si cresce in civiltà, che sola in meglio
Guida i pubblici fati.
Così ti spiacque il vero
Dell'aspra sorte e del depresso loco
Che natura ci diè. Per questo il tergo
70 Vigliaccamente rivolgesti al lume
Che il fe' palese: e, fuggitivo, appelli
Vil chi lui segue, e solo
Magnanimo colui
Che sé schernendo o gli altri, astuto o folle,
75 Fin sopra gli astri il mortal grado estolle.

Uom di povero stato e membra inferme
Che sia dell'alma generoso ed alto,
Non chiama sé né stima
Ricco d'or né gagliardo,
80 E di splendida vita o di valente
Persona infra la gente
Non fa risibil mostra;
Ma sé di forza e di tesor mendico
Lascia parer senza vergogna, e noma
85 Parlando, apertamente, e di sue cose
Fa stima al vero uguale.
Magnanimo animale
Non credo io già, ma stolto,
Quel che nato a perir, nutrito in pene,
Dice, a goder son fatto,
90 E di fetido orgoglio
Empie le carte, eccelsi fati e nove

The man too bitterly opposed
To his own time. By now, however,
I can laugh at this misfortune
Which makes us equal in the end.
Freedom is the dream you dream
While putting thought in chains again—
Thought, which is all that brought us
Almost out of the barbarous dark, alone
Enabled civilization, is what alone
Steers the state toward a better life.
Having no love for the bitter truth
Of that hard lot and lowly place
Which nature gave us, you turned
Your coward's back on the light
That lets us see these things as they are,
And deserting it yourself you chide
As churlish any man who'd guide
His life by it, proclaiming as great of soul
Only him—crazy or cunning,
Hoodwinking himself or others—
Who'll praise our mortal state above the stars.

A man of poor health and little means
Who has a decent, open spirit
Won't pretend he's robust or rich
Nor make a silly show of himself
By living the gallant life
Of a man of the world.
He, without any shame, will show
His own lack of strength and substance,
Openly admitting the whole truth
Just of who and what he is.
And I myself don't ever deem
A creature great of soul,
But only a fool,
That man who—bred in pain, born to die—
Declares, *I was made to be happy,*
And fills page after scribbled page
With the stink of pride,

Felicità, quali il ciel tutto ignora,
Non pur quest'orbe, promettendo in terra
A popoli che un'onda
95   Di mar commosso, un fiato
D'aura maligna, un sotterraneo crollo
Distrugge sì, che avanza
A gran pena di lor la rimembranza.
Nobil natura è quella
100   Ch'a sollevar s'ardisce
Gli occhi mortali incontra
Al comun fato, e che con franca lingua,
Nulla al ver detraendo,
Confessa il mal che ci fu dato in sorte,
105   E il basso stato e frale;
Quella che grande e forte
Mostra sé nel soffrir, né gli odii e l'ire
Fraterne, ancor più gravi
D'ogni altro danno, accresce
110   Alle miserie sue, l'uomo incolpando
Del suo dolor, ma dà la colpa a quella
Che veramente è rea, che de' mortali
Madre è di parto e di voler matrigna.
Costei chiama inimica; e incontro a questa
115   Congiunta esser pensando,
Siccom'è il vero, ed ordinata in pria
L'umana compagnia,
Tutti fra sé confederati estima
Gli uomini, e tutti abbraccia
120   Con vero amor, porgendo
Valida e pronta ed aspettando aita
Negli alterni perigli e nelle angosce
Della guerra comune. Ed alle offese
Dell'uomo armar la destra, e laccio porre
125   Al vicino ed inciampo,
Stolto crede così, qual fora in campo
Cinto d'oste contraria, in sul più vivo
Incalzar degli assalti,
Gl'inimici obbliando, acerbe gare
130   Imprender con gli amici,

Promising on earth
Such fortunes sublime and miracles of joy
As heaven itself—not to mention
The world we live in—couldn't encompass,
And all this to creatures wiped away
By a single shaken wave of the sea,
Snatched off by a sudden wicked gust of wind,
So annihilated by an underground tremor
There'd be little or nothing left to remember.
That man has a *truly* noble nature
Who, without flinching, still can face
Our common plight, tell the truth
With an honest tongue,
Admit the evil lot we've been given
And the abject, impotent condition we're in;
Who shows himself great and full of grace
Under pressure, not adding to his miseries
The hate and hostility of his fellow-men
(And what hurt could be worse than these?)
By blaming man for his distress,
But lays the blame where it belongs—on her
Who is a mother in giving us life,
A wicked stepmother in how she treats us.
She's the one he calls the enemy,
And believing the human family
Leagued to oppose her, as in truth it is
And has been from the start, he sees
As allies all men, embraces all
With unfeigned love, giving and expecting
Prompt assistance, useful aid
In the many hazards and lasting hurts
Of the common struggle. And he believes
It sheer madness
To arm your hand against another,
Lay snares or stumbling blocks for your neighbor,
As mad as, in a state of siege—
Surrounded by enemies, the assault at its height—
To forget the foe and in blind rage
Turn your force upon your friends,

E sparger fuga e fulminar col brando
Infra i propri guerrieri.
Così fatti pensieri
Quando fien, come fur, palesi al volgo,
135    E quell'orror che primo
Contra l'empia natura
Strinse i mortali in social catena,
Fia ricondotto in parte
Da verace saper, l'onesto e il retto
140    Conversar cittadino,
E giustizia e pietade, altra radice
Avranno allor che non superbe fole,
Ove fondata probità del volgo
Così star suole in piede
145    Quale star può quel c'ha in error la sede.


Sovente in queste rive,
Che, desolate, a bruno
Veste il flutto indurato, e par che ondeggi,
Seggo la notte; e su la mesta landa
150    In purissimo azzurro
Veggo dall'alto fiammeggiar le stelle,
Cui di lontan fa specchio
Il mare, e tutto di scintille in giro
Per lo vòto seren brillare il mondo.
155    E poi che gli occhi a quelle luci appunto,
Ch'a lor sembrano un punto,
E sono immense, in guisa
Che un punto a petto a lor son terra e mare
Veracemente; a cui
160    L'uomo non pur, ma questo
Globo ove l'uomo è nulla,
Sconosciuto è del tutto; e quando miro
Quegli ancor più senz'alcun fin remoti
Nodi quasi di stelle,
165    Ch'a noi paion qual nebbia, a cui non l'uomo
E non la terra sol, ma tutte in uno,
Del numero infinite e della mole,
Con l'aureo sole insiem, le nostre stelle

Smite with the sword, sow havoc and panic
Amongst those fighting on your own side.
When ideas such as these are clear,
As once they were, to the common people,
And when the terror that first forged
For human beings the social bond
Against the savagery of nature
Shall, in part, be again restored
By a true grasp of things as they are, then
Justice and mercy
And an open, honest civil life
Will no longer take root in those swollen fables
On which our stolid common morals
Are mostly grounded, and where they stand
As steady as anything built on sand.

Often I sit out at night
On these forlorn slopes
Which the undulant rough crust of lava
Turns dark brown, and I see
In the clear blue evening sky the stars
Blazing down on the melancholy scene
And in the distant mirror made by the sea,
Until the whole world seems
All one gleaming orb of sparks
Floating through a perfect void.
And when I peer out at those lights
That seem no more than specks from here
But are in fact so huge that truly
Land and sea are specks to them,
Where not just man himself but this
Great globe where man is nothing
Isn't known at all; and when I gaze on out
At those infinitely more remote
Clusters of stars that look like clouds,
To which not merely man, not earth,
But all our stars together, numberless
And vaster than we can imagine,
The golden sun itself among them,

O sono ignote, o così paion come
170   Essi alla terra, un punto
Di luce nebulosa; al pensier mio
Che sembri allora, o prole
Dell'uomo? E rimembrando
Il tuo stato quaggiù, di cui fa segno
175   Il suol ch'io premo; e poi dall'altra parte,
Che te signora e fine
Credi tu data al Tutto; e quante volte
Favoleggiar ti piacque, in questo oscuro
Granel di sabbia, il qual di terra ha nome,
180   Per tua cagion, dell'universe cose
Scender gli autori, e conversar sovente
Co' tuoi piacevolmente, e che, i derisi
Sogni rinnovellando, ai saggi insulta
Fin la presente età, che in conoscenza
185   Ed in civil costume
Sembra tutte avanzar; qual moto allora,
Mortal prole infelice, o qual pensiero
Verso te finalmente il cor m'assale?
Non so se il riso o la pietà prevale.

190   Come d'arbor cadendo un picciol pomo,
Cui là nel tardo autunno
Maturità senz'altra forza atterra,
D'un popol di formiche i dolci alberghi,
Cavati in molle gleba
195   Con gran lavoro, e l'opre
E le ricchezze ch'adunate a prova
Con lungo affaticar l'assidua gente
Avea provvidamente al tempo estivo,
Schiaccia, diserta e copre
200   In un punto; così d'alto piombando,
Dall'utero tonante
Scagliata al ciel profondo,

Are either invisible or else appear
As those clusters themselves appear
To us on earth—just a smudge
Of cloudy light—then what can I make
Of you, my family of man? And when
I consider your earthly state
(Its very sign the ground I stand on)
And how, in spite of it, you still
Take for granted you've been made
Lord and measure and end of all,
And the many times you've loved to tell
Fables and fairy tales of how
On your behalf even the authors
Of the universe itself came down
To this dark grain of sand called earth,
And how, time after time, they talked
With you on friendly terms, and how
Over and over you've told these same
Silly dreams, insulting men of any sense
Even into the present age
That seems advanced beyond all others
In knowledge and norms of civil life—
When I consider you, then,
Wretched race of mortal men,
What thoughts batter my heart? I
Cannot tell whether to laugh or cry.

Just as a little apple falling
From the tree in late autumn—
Which no force but ripeness alone brings down—
Crushes, lays waste, and buries in an instant
Those neat dwellings the ants have labored
To fashion in the soft clay,
Destroying all the precious stores
These painstaking, driven creatures
Had prudently harvested
Over the months of summer, so—
Flung from the mountain's
Thundering bowels to the wide sky

Di ceneri e di pomici e di sassi
Notte e ruina, infusa
205 Di bollenti ruscelli,
O pel montano fianco
Furiosa tra l'erba
Di liquefatti massi
E di metalli e d'infocata arena
210 Scendendo immensa piena,
Le cittadi che il mar là su l'estremo
Lido aspergea, confuse
E infranse e ricoperse
In pochi istanti: onde su quelle or pasce
215 La capra, e città nove
Sorgon dall'altra banda, a cui sgabello
Son le sepolte, e le prostrate mura
L'arduo monte al suo piè quasi calpesta.
Non ha natura al seme
220 Dell'uom più stima o cura
Ch'alla formica: e se più rara in quello
Che nell'altra è la strage,
Non avvien ciò d'altronde
Fuor che l'uom sue prosapie ha men feconde.

225 Ben mille ed ottocento
Anni varcàr poi che spariro, oppressi
Dall'ignea forza, i popolati seggi,
E il villanello intento
Ai vigneti, che a stento in questi campi
230 Nutre la morta zolla e incenerita,
Ancor leva lo sguardo
Sospettoso alla vetta
Fatal, che nulla mai fatta più mite
Ancor siede tremenda, ancor minaccia
240 A lui strage ed ai figli ed agli averi
Lor poverelli. E spesso
Il meschino in sul tetto
Dell'ostel villereccio, alla vagante
Aura giacendo tutta notte insonne,

And plummeting from a great height—
A downpour black as night
Of ashes, brimstone, boulders
With boiling streams of lava riddled,
Or a flood of molten
Rock, metal, blazing sand
Torn through the mountain's side and thrown
In a crazy spate through tall grass
Once overwhelmed, shattered to bits,
And buried in seconds these coastal towns
Washed by the waves of the sea,
So that now, goats browse above them
And new towns rise on the far side
Which have as their footstool
Those razed and buried walls
The sheer-sloped mountain
All but tramples in the dust.
For nature has no
Kinder regard for man
Than she has for ants, and if such slaughters
Don't befall us as often, the only reason
Is our loins breed
Less than the loins of those teeming creatures.

It's almost eighteen hundred years
Since these thriving towns
Were wiped out by the force of fire,
And still the peasant tending his vines—
Which the thin, cinder-choked soil
Can barely sustain—will cast
Wary glances up
At that death-dealing peak, no gentler
Now than ever, still a terror-
Striking sight, still threatening
Death and destruction to him and his children
And their few poor possessions.
And oftentimes, out on the roof of his cottage,
This wretch will bend all night
A sleepless ear to the shifting

245 E balzando più volte, esplora il corso
    Del temuto bollor, che si riversa
    Dall' inesausto grembo
    Sull'arenoso dorso, a cui riluce
    Di Capri la marina
250 E di Napoli il porto e Mergellina.
    E se appressar lo vede, o se nel cupo
    Del domestico pozzo ode mai l'acqua
    Fervendo gorgogliar, desta i figliuoli,
    Desta la moglie in fretta, e via, con quanto
255 Di lor cose rapir posson, fuggendo,
    Vede lontan l'usato
    Suo nido, e il picciol campo
    Che gli fu dalla fame unico schermo,
    Preda al flutto rovente,
260 Che crepitando giunge, e inesorato
    Durabilmente sovra quei si spiega.
    Torna al celeste raggio
    Dopo l'antica obblivion l'estinta
    Pompei, come sepolto
265 Scheletro, cui di terra
    Avarizia o pietà rende all'aperto;
    E dal deserto foro
    Diritto infra le file
    Dei mozzi colonnati il peregrino
270 Lunge contempla il bipartito giogo
    E la cresta fumante,
    Che alla sparsa ruina ancor minaccia.
    E nell'orror della secreta notte
    Per li vacui teatri,
275 Per li templi deformi e per le rotte
    Case, ove i parti il pipistrello asconde,
    Come sinistra face
    Che per vòti palagi atra s'aggiri,
    Corre il baglior della funerea lava,
280 Che di lontan per l'ombre
    Rosseggia e i lochi intorno intorno tinge.
    Così, dell'uomo ignara e dell'etadi
    Ch'ei chiama antiche, e del seguir che fanno

Sound of the wind, many times
Starting to his feet to mark
The fearful track the lava makes
As it pours from infinitely brimming bowels
Over the mountain's naked back,
Lighting up the whole coast
Of Capri, and Mergellina, and the port of Naples.
And if he sees it getting closer, or hears
The watery black depths of his well
Gurgling like a mad thing, he'll rouse his children,
Shake his wife awake, and fleeing
With whatever they can snatch up,
He'll see from a safe distance
His hearth and home and that patch of ground
He had to keep hunger from the door
Fall prey to the red-hot torrent
That comes with a great crackling roar
And, relentless and forever, smothers everything.
Obliterated for ages, forgotten Pompeii
Like a buried skeleton—which greed for treasure
Or respect for the dead lays bare—
Rises to the blessed light of day;
And from that deserted forum
A traveler will stare for a long time
Out between rows of broken columns
And up at the cloven summit
And smoking crest
That still threaten these scattered ruins.
And in the dread dead of night
Through the empty theatres,
Through shattered temples and the remains
Of houses where the bat hides its young,
The grim lava-glow goes floating
Like an eerie torch that flickers
Among abandoned palaces,
And from far away reddens the darkness
And stains every place in sight.
So—indifferent to men and what men call
Antiquity, to all the ties that bind

Dopo gli avi i nepoti,
285 Sta natura ognor verde, anzi procede
Per sì lungo cammino
Che sembra star. Caggiono i regni intanto,
Passan genti e linguaggi: ella nol vede:
E l'uom d'eternità s'arroga il vanto.

290 E tu, lenta ginestra,
Che di selve odorate
Queste campagne dispogliate adorni,
Anche tu presto alla crudel possanza
Soccomberai del sotterraneo foco,
295 Che ritornando al loco
Già noto, stenderà l'avaro lembo
Su tue molli foreste. E piegherai
Sotto il fascio mortal non renitente
Il tuo capo innocente:
300 Ma non piegato insino allora indarno
Codardamente supplicando innanzi
Al futuro oppressor; ma non eretto
Con forsennato orgoglio inver le stelle,
Né sul deserto, dove
305 E la sede e i natali
Non per voler ma per fortuna avesti;
Ma più saggia, ma tanto
Meno inferma dell'uom, quanto le frali
Tue stirpi non credesti
310 O dal fato o da te fatte immortali.

1836

One generation to another—nature
Stays forever green, or seems,
Having so vast a path to travel,
To stay still forever. Meantime, kingdoms perish,
Nations and the tongues of nations
Pass away: nothing of this at all she'll see:
And man boasts he owns eternity

And even you, delicate hedges of broom,
Who bless this desolation
With groves of fragrance,
Even you will succumb soon enough
To the tyranny of fire from underground.
Returning to its old haunts,
The fire will spread its deadly mantle
Over your tender hedgerows; then,
Beneath its fatal weight you'll bend
Your innocent, unresisting heads. But
Till that time comes you won't bow down
Like cowards before the one who'll destroy you,
Seeking your salvation in vain; and you won't
Raise vainglorious heads to the stars
Or up above this wasteland where
By chance and not by choice you have
Your birthplace and your home; and still
You're wiser and that much less weak
Than man, inasmuch as you don't believe
These delicate stems of yours have been,
By yourself or the fatal scheme
Of things, fashioned for immortality.

# The Lockert Library of Poetry in Translation

*George Seferis: Collected Poems (1924–1955)*, translated, edited, and introduced by Edmund Keeley and Philip Sherrard

*Collected Poems of Lucio Piccolo*, translated and edited by Brian Swann and Ruth Feldman

*C. P. Cavafy: Collected Poems*, translated by Edmund Keeley and Philip Sherrard and edited by George Savidis

*Benny Andersen: Selected Poems*, translated by Alexander Taylor

*Selected Poetry of Andrea Zanzotto*, edited and translated by Ruth Feldman and Brian Swann

*Poems of René Char*, translated and annnotated by Mary Ann Caws and Jonathan Griffin

*Selected Poems of Tudor Arghezi*, translated by Michale Impey and Brian Swann

*"The Survivor" and Other Poems* by Tadeusz Różewicz, translated and introduced by Magnus J. Krynski and Robert A. Maguire

*"Harsh World" and Other Poems* by Angel González, translated by Donald D. Walsh

*Ritsos in Parentheses*, translations and introduction by Edmund Keeley

*Salamander: Selected Poems of Robert Marteau*, translated by Anne Winters

*Angelos Sikelianos: Selected Poems*, translated and introduced by Edmund Keeley and Philip Sherrard

*Dante's "Rime,"* translated by Patrick Diehl

*Selected Later Poems of Marie Luise Kashnitz*, translated by Lisel Mueller

*Osip Mandelstam's "Stone,"* translated and introduced by Robert Tracy

*The Dawn Is Always New: Selected Poetry of Rocco Scotellaro*, translated by Ruth Feldman and Brian Swann

*Sounds, Feelings, Thoughts: Seventy Poems by Wisława Szymborska*, translated and introduced by Magnus J. Krynski and Robert A. Maguire

*The Man I Pretend to Be: "The Colloquies" and Selected Poems of Guido Gozzano*, translated and edited by Michael Palma, with an introductory essay by Eugenio Montale

*D'Après Tout: Poems by Jean Follain,* translated by Heather McHugh

*Songs of Something Else: Selected Poems of Gunnar Ekelöf,* translated by Leonard Nathan and James Larson

*The Little Treasury of One Hundred People, One Poem Each,* compiled by Fujiwara No Sadaie and translated by Tom Galt

*The Ellipse: Selected Poems of Leonardo Sinisgalli,* translated by W. S. Di Piero

*The Difficult Days* by Roberto Sosa, translated by Jim Lindsey

*Hymns and Fragments* by Friedrich Hölderlin, transalted and introduced by Richard Sieburth

*The Silence Afterwards: Selected Poems of Rolf Jacobsen,* translated and edited by Roger Greenwald

*Rilke: Between Roots,* selected poems rendered from the German by Rika Lesser

*In the Storm of Roses: Selected Poems by Ingeborg Bachmann,* translated, edited, and introduced by Mark Anderson

*Birds and Other Relations: Selected Poetry of Dezső Tandori,* translated by Bruce Berlind

*Brocade River Poems: Selected Works of the Tang Dynasty Courtesan Xue Tao,* translated and introduced by Jeanne Larsen

*The True Subject: Selected Poems of Faiz Ahmed Faiz,* translated by Naomi Lazard

*My Name on the Wind: Selected Poems of Diego Valeri,* translated by Michael Palma

*Aeschylus: The Suppliants,* translated by Peter Burian

*Foamy Sky: The Major Poems of Miklós Radnóti,* selected and translated by Zsuzsanna Ozsváth and Frederick Turner

*La Fontaine's Bawdy: Of Libertines, Louts, and Lechers,* translated by Norman R. Shapiro

*A Child Is Not a Knife: Selected Poems of Göran Sonnevi,* translated and edited by Rika Lesser

*George Seferis: Collected Poems, Revised Edition,* translated, edited and introduced by Edmund Keeley and Philip Sherrard

*C. P. Cavafy: Collected Poems, Revised Edition,* translated and introduced by Edmund Keeley and Philip Sherrard, and edited by George Savidis

*The Late Poems of Meng Chiao*, translated and introduced by David Hinton

*Leopardi: Selected Poems*, translated and introduced by Eamon Grennan

*The Complete Odes and Satires of Horace*, translated with introduction and notes by Sidney Alexander